CW01658942

THE GRAVE

ITS TORMENT AND ITS PLEASURE

BY SHAYKH MUHAMMAD AL-WASAABEE

ISBN: 978-1-4675-9235-2

First Edition: Rajab 1435 A.H. / May 2014 C.E.

Cover Design: Usul Design

E-mail: info@usuldesign.com

Translator: Ihsân Ibn Gerald Gonsalves

Typesetting & Formatting: Abu Sulaymaan Muhammad Abdul-Azim Ibn Baker

E-mail: maktabatulirshad@gmail.com

Publisher's Information:

Authentic Statements Publishing
P.O.Box 15536
Phila, Pa. 19131
215.382-3382
215.382.3782-Fax

Store:

5000 Locust St.(Side Entrance)
Phila Pa 19139

Website: www.authenticstatements.com

E-mail: info@authenticstatements.com

Please visit our website for upcoming publications, audio/Dvd online catalog, and info on events and seminars, insha Allah.

Table of Contents

INTRODUCTION

All praise is due to the Lord of Creation and may the blessings and peace be upon the most noble of the messengers, our Prophet Muhammad, may Allah bless him and bestow peace upon him, his family, and his companions.

As for what follows:

I gathered in this humble research the verses of the book of Allah, the hadith of His prophet's sunnah (sallallahu alaihi wa sallam) and proof of what was the belief of Ahlus Sunnah wal Jama'ah regarding the torment and bliss of the grave, and how it differs from the belief of the misguided groups from amongst the people of innovation and desires.

Indeed, it is the first stage that the slave proceeds to after the worldly life. In it, the people of Al-Barzakh will find what they deserve of torment or bliss, depending on their state in the dunya, and then to Heaven or the Hell-fire, and therein will reside in the never-ending residence.

We ask Allah, the Most High, to make it sincerely for His Face and that it becomes a cause for the unheeding to take heed and awaken the sleeping, so that they may be saved from Allah's punishment, and that it may be a cause for the righteous to increase in good deeds until they obtain Allah's mercy.

Likewise, we ask Him, the Glorified, to bless us with Heaven and the speech and actions that draw a person close to it. We seek refuge in Him from the Fire and the speech and actions that draw a person close to it. Verily, He's All-Hearing, near, and responsive.

May Allah bless our prophet Muhammad, his family and companions, and send upon them abundant peace.

Abu Ibrahim Muhammad bin Abdul-Wahhab Al-Wasabi

CHAPTER ONE: THE QURANIC VERSES

1. Allah, the Most High, said:

﴿ وَمَنْ أَظْلَمُ مِمَّنِ افْتَرَىٰ عَلَى اللَّهِ كَذِبًا أَوْ قَالَ أُوحِيَ إِلَيَّ وَلَمْ يُوحَ إِلَيْهِ
شَيْءٌ وَمَن قَالَ سَأُنزِلُ مِثْلَ مَا أَنزَلَ اللَّهُ ۗ وَلَوْ تَرَىٰ إِذِ الظَّالِمُونَ فِي
غَمَرَاتِ الْمَوْتِ وَالْمَلَائِكَةُ بَاسِطُو أَيْدِيهِمْ أَخْرِجُوا أَنفُسَكُمُ ۖ الْيَوْمَ
تُجْزَوْنَ عَذَابَ الْهُونِ بِمَا كُنتُمْ تَقُولُونَ عَلَى اللَّهِ غَيْرَ الْحَقِّ وَكُنتُمْ
عَنْ آيَاتِهِ تَسْتَكْبِرُونَ ﴿٩٣﴾ ﴾

"And if you could but see when the *dhalimun* (polytheists and wrong-doers, etc.) are in the agonies of death, while the angels are stretching forth their hands (saying): 'Deliver your souls! This day you shall be recompensed with the torment of degradation because of what you used to utter against Allah other than the truth. And you used to reject His ayat (proofs, evidences, verses, lessons, signs, revelations, etc.) with disrespect!'" [1]

2. Allah, the Most High, said:

---

[1] Soorah Al-An'am (6:93)

﴿ وَمِمَّنْ حَوْلَكُم مِّنَ ٱلْأَعْرَابِ مُنَٰفِقُونَ ۖ وَمِنْ أَهْلِ ٱلْمَدِينَةِ ۖ مَرَدُوا۟ عَلَى
ٱلنِّفَاقِ لَا تَعْلَمُهُمْ ۖ نَحْنُ نَعْلَمُهُمْ ۚ سَنُعَذِّبُهُم مَّرَّتَيْنِ ثُمَّ يُرَدُّونَ إِلَىٰ عَذَابٍ
عَظِيمٍ ﴿١٠١﴾ ﴾

"And among the Bedouins round about you, some are hypocrites, and so are some among the people of Al-Madinah, they exaggerate and persist in hypocrisy, you know them not, We know them. We shall punish them twice, and thereafter they shall be brought back to a great torment." [2]

3. Allah, the Most High, said:

﴿ فَوَقَىٰهُ ٱللَّهُ سَيِّـَٔاتِ مَا مَكَرُوا۟ ۖ وَحَاقَ بِـَٔالِ فِرْعَوْنَ سُوٓءُ ٱلْعَذَابِ ﴿٤٥﴾
ٱلنَّارُ يُعْرَضُونَ عَلَيْهَا غُدُوًّا وَعَشِيًّا ۖ وَيَوْمَ تَقُومُ ٱلسَّاعَةُ أَدْخِلُوٓا۟ ءَالَ فِرْعَوْنَ
أَشَدَّ ٱلْعَذَابِ ﴿٤٦﴾ ﴾

"So Allah saved him from the evils that they plotted (against him), while an evil torment encompassed Fir'aun's people. The Fire; they are exposed to it, morning and afternoon, and on the Day when the Hour will be established (it will be said to the

---

2 Soorah At-Taubah (9:101)

angels): 'Cause Fir'aun's people to enter the severest torment!'" [3]

4. Allah, the Most High, said:

﴿فَإِنَّ لَهُۥ مَعِيشَةً ضَنكًا وَنَحْشُرُهُۥ يَوْمَ ٱلْقِيَٰمَةِ أَعْمَىٰ ١٢٤﴾

"Verily, for him is a life of hardship, and We shall raise him up blind on the Day of Resurrection." [4]

5. Allah, the Most High, said:

﴿يُثَبِّتُ ٱللَّهُ ٱلَّذِينَ ءَامَنُوا۟ بِٱلْقَوْلِ ٱلثَّابِتِ فِى ٱلْحَيَوٰةِ ٱلدُّنْيَا وَفِى
ٱلْءَاخِرَةِ ۖ﴾

"Allah will keep firm those who believe, with the word that stands firm in this world (i.e., they will keep on worshipping Allah Alone and none else), and in the Hereafter." [5]

6. Allah, the Most High, said:

﴿وَلَنُذِيقَنَّهُم مِّنَ ٱلْعَذَابِ ٱلْأَدْنَىٰ دُونَ ٱلْعَذَابِ ٱلْأَكْبَرِ لَعَلَّهُمْ
يَرْجِعُونَ ٢١﴾

---

[3] Soorah Ghafir (40: 45-46)
[4] Soorah Ta-Ha (20:124)
[5] Soorah Ibrahim (14:27)

"And verily, We will make them taste of the near torment prior to the supreme torment, in order that they may return." [6]

7. Allah, the Most High, said:

﴿ وَإِنَّ لِلَّذِينَ ظَلَمُوا۟ عَذَابًا دُونَ ذَٰلِكَ وَلَٰكِنَّ أَكْثَرَهُمْ لَا يَعْلَمُونَ ﴿٤٧﴾ ﴾

"And verily, for those who do wrong, there is another punishment before this, but most of them know not."[7]

---

[6] Soorah As-Sajdah (32: 21)

[7] Soorah At-Tur (52: 47)

CHAPTER 2: THE PLEASURE OF THE GRAVE

1. It is related from Abu Hurayrah (radiallahu anhu) that the Messenger of Allah (sallallahu alaihi wa sallam) said:

إِنَّ الْمُؤْمِنَ فِي قَبْرِهِ، لَفِي رَوْضَةٍ خَضْرَاءَ ، فَيُرَحَّبُ لَهُ فِي قَبْرِهِ سَبْعِينَ ذِرَاعًا ، وَ يُنَوَّرُ لَهُ كَالْقَمَرِ لَيْلَةَ الْبَدْرِ. أَ تَدْرُونَ فِيمَ أُنْزِلَتْ هَذِهِ الآيَةُ : ﴿ فَإِنَّ لَهُۥ مَعِيشَةً ضَنكًا وَنَحْشُرُهُۥ يَوْمَ ٱلْقِيَٰمَةِ أَعْمَىٰ ﴿١٢٤﴾ ﴾ أَ تَدْرُونَ مَا الْمَعِيشَةُ الضَّنْكُ ؟ قَالُوا : اللهُ وَ رَسُولُهُ أَعْلَمُ. قَالَ : ((عَذَابُ الْكَافِرِ فِي قَبْرِهِ، وَ الَّذِي نَفْسِي بِيَدِهِ، إِنَّهُ يُسَلَّطُ عَلَيْهِ تِسْعَةٌ وَ تِسْعُونَ تِنِّينًا ، أَ تَدْرُونَ مَا التِّنِّينُ ؟! تِسْعُونَ حَيَّةً ، لِكُلِّ حَيَّةٍ سَبْعُ رُؤُوسٍ ، يَلْسَعُونَهُ، وَ يَخْدِشُونَهُ إِلَى يَوْمِ الْقِيَامَةِ .

"Verily, the believer in his grave is in a green garden. For his sake, his grave is widened seventy arm lengths and it is lit up for him like the light of the full moon. Do you know why this verse was revealed: 'Verily, for him is a life of hardship, and We shall raise him up blind on the Day of

Resurrection?' Do you know the meaning of 'for him is a life of hardship'? They said: 'Allah and His messenger knows best.' He said: 'That is the punishment of the disbeliever in his grave. By the One in Whose Hand is my soul, ninety nine *tinneen* are set upon him. Do you know what a *tinneen* is? Ninety nine snakes and every snake has seven heads. They bite and scratch him till the Day of Resurrection.'" [8]

2. It is related from Jabir bin Abdullah Al-Ansari that he related that the Prophet (sallallahu alaihi wa sallam) said:

إِذَا رَأَى الْمُؤْمِنُ مَا فُسِحَ لَهُ فِي قَبْرِهِ، يَقُولُ : دَعُونِي أُبَشِّرُ أَهْلِي . فَيُقَالُ لَهُ: اُسْكُنْ .

"When the believer sees how his grave has been made wide for him, he will say: 'Let me return to my family so I can inform them.' Then he will be told: 'Rest'."

3. It is related from Abu Qatada (radiallahu anhu) who said that a funeral passed by the Messenger of Allah (sallallahu alaihi wa sallam) and he said:

[8] Reported by Abu Ya'la and Ibn Hiban. Sheikh Al-Albani (rahimahullah) declared it to be good in "Sahih At-Targib wa At-Tarhib, number: 3552.

مُسْتَرِيحٌ ، وَ مُسْتَرَاحٌ مِنْهُ . قَالُوا : يَا رَسُولَ اللهِ ، مَا الْمُسْتَرِيحُ ؟ وَ مَا الْمُسْتَرَاحُ مِنْهُ ؟ قَالَ : ((الْعَبْدُ الْمُؤْمِنُ : يَسْتَرِيحُ مِنْ نَصَبِ الدُّنْيَا ، وَ أَذَاهَا ، إِلَى رَحْمَةِ اللهِ ، وَ الْعَبْدُ الْفَاجِرُ : يَسْتَرِيحُ مِنْهُ الْعِبَادُ ، وَ الْبِلَادُ ، وَالشَّجَرُ ، وَ الدَّوَابُّ)) .

"Relieved and relieving." They asked: "Messenger of Allah, what is relieved and relieving?" He said: "The believing slave is relieved from the troubles and hardships of the world and leaves for the Mercy of Allah, while the wicked slave relieves the people, the land, the trees, and the animals from him." [9]

4. It is related from Abu Hurayrah that the Prophet (sallallahu alaihi wa sallam) said:

أَسْرِعُوا بِالْجِنَازَةِ ، فَإِنْ تَكُ صَالِحَةً ، فَخَيْرٌ تُقَدِّمُونَهَا ، وَ إِنْ يَكُ سِوَى ذَلِكَ ، فَشَرٌّ تَضَعُونَهُ عَنْ رِقَابِكُمْ .

"Carry the deceased quickly. If he was righteous, it is good you are advancing him to. If he was other

[9] Reported by Al-Bukhari, number: 6147 and 6148; and Muslim, number: 950.

than that, then it is an evil you are removing from your necks." [10]

5. It is related from A'ishah that she said: "The Messenger of Allah (sallallahu alaihi wa sallam) said:

مَنْ أَحَبَّ لِقَاءَ اللهِ ، أَحَبَّ اللهُ لِقَاءَهُ ، وَ مَنْ كَرِهَ لِقَاءَ اللهِ ، كَرِهَ اللهُ لِقَاءَهُ . فَقُلْتُ : يَا نَبِيَّ اللهِ ، أَ كَرَاهِيَةُ الْمَوْتِ ؟ فَكُلُّنَا نَكْرَهُ الْمَوْتَ . فَقَالَ : ((لَيْسَ كَذَلِكَ ، وَ لَكِنَّ الْمُؤْمِنَ إِذَا بُشِّرَ بِرَحْمَةِ اللهِ ، وَ رِضْوَانِهِ ، وَ جَنَّتِهِ ، أَحَبَّ لِقَاءَ اللهِ ، فَأَحَبَّ اللهُ لِقَاءَهُ ، وَ إِنَّ الْكَافِرَ إِذَا بُشِّرَ بِعَذَابِ اللهِ ، وَ سَخَطِهِ، كَرِهَ لِقَاءَ اللهِ ، وَ كَرِهَ اللهُ لِقَاءَهُ .

'He who loves to meet Allah, Allah loves to meet him, and he who dislikes to meet Allah, Allah dislikes to meet him.' So I said: 'Oh Prophet of Allah, regarding the dislike of death, we all dislike death.' Then he said: 'It's not like that, rather, when the believer is given the good news of the mercy of Allah and His pleasure and His garden, he wants to meet Allah and so Allah wants to meet him. But when the unbeliever is given the news of the punishment of Allah and His wrath, then he

---

[10] Reported by Al-Bukhari, number: 1252; and Muslim, number: 944.

dislikes to meet Allah and so Allah dislikes meeting him.'" [11]

6. It is related from Umm Salama that the Messenger of Allah (sallallahu alaihi wa sallam) came to Abu Salama. His eyes were fixed open. He closed them, and then said:

إِنَّ الرُّوحَ إِذَا قُبِضَ ، تَبِعَهُ الْبَصَرُ . فَضَجَّ نَاسٌ مِنْ أَهْلِهِ ، فَقَالَ : ((لَا تَدْعُوا عَلَى أَنْفُسِكُمْ إِلَّا بِخَيْرٍ ، فَإِنَّ الْمَلَائِكَةَ يُؤَمِّنُونَ عَلَى مَا تَقُولُونَ)) . ثُمَّ قَالَ : ((اللَّهُمَّ اغْفِرْ لِأَبِي سَلَمَةَ ، وَارْفَعْ دَرَجَتَهُ فِي الْمَهْدِيِّينَ ، وَاخْلُفْهُ فِي عَقِبِهِ فِي الْغَابِرِينَ ، وَاغْفِرْ لَنَا ، وَ لَهُ يَا رَبَّ الْعَالَمِينَ ! وَافْسَحْ لَهُ فِي قَبْرِهِ ، وَ نَوِّرْ لَهُ فِيهِ .))

"When the soul is taken away, the sight follows it." Some of the people of his family wept and wailed. So he said: "Do not supplicate for yourselves anything but good, for the angels say 'Ameen' to what you say." He then said: "Oh Allah, forgive Abu Salama, raise his rank amongst the rightly guided, grant him a successor from amongst his descendants who remain behind. Forgive us and

[11] Reported by Al-Bukhari, number: 6142; and Muslim, number: 2684 and 2685, and the wording is his.

him, Oh Lord of creation, and make his grave spacious, and grant him light in it." [12]

7. It is related from Al-Bara bin Aazib who said:

خَرَجْنَا مَعَ النَّبِيِّ ، صَلَّى اللهُ عَلَيْهِ وَسَلَّمَ ، فِي جِنَازَةِ رَجُلٍ مِنَ الأَنْصَارِ . قَالَ : فَانْتَهَيْنَا إِلَى الْقَبْرِ ، وَلَمَّا يَلْحَدْ . قَالَ : فَجَلَسَ رَسُولُ اللهِّ ، صَلَّى اللهُ عَلَيْهِ وَسَلَّمَ ، وَجَلَسْنَا حَوْلَهُ كَأَنَّ عَلَى رُءُوسِنَا الطَّيْرَ ، وَفِي يَدِهِ عُودٌ يَنْكُتُ بِهِ الأَرْضَ . قَالَ : فَرَفَعَ رَأْسَهُ ، فَقَالَ((: اسْتَعِيذُوا بِاللهِ مِنْ عَذَابِ الْقَبْرِ ، اسْتَعِيذُوا بِاللهِ مِنْ عَذَابِ الْقَبْرِ)) . مَرَّتَيْنِ أَوْ ثَلاثًا . ثُمَّ قَالَ : ((إِنَّ الْعَبْدَ الْمُؤْمِنَ إِذَا كَانَ فِي انْقِطَاعٍ مِنَ الدُّنْيَا ، وَإِقْبَالٍ مِنَ الآخِرَةِ ؛ نَزَّلَ اللهُ ، تَبَارَكَ وَتَعَالَى ، مَلائِكَةً مِنَ السَّمَاءِ بِيضَ الْوُجُوهِ ، كَأَنَّ وُجُوهَهُمُ الشَّمْسُ ، مَعَهُمْ كَفَنٌ مِنْ أَكْفَانِ الْجَنَّةِ ، وَحَنُوطٌ مِنْ حَنُوطِ الْجَنَّةِ حَتَّى يَجْلِسُونَ مِنْهُ مَدَّ الْبَصَرِ . ثُمَّ يَجِيءُ مَلَكُ الْمَوْتِ ، صَلَّى اللهُ عَلَيْهِ وَسَلَّمَ ، حَتَّى يَجْلِسَ عَلَى رَأْسِهِ فَيَقُولُ : أَيَّتُهَا النَّفْسُ الطَّيِّبَةُ ، اخْرُجِي إِلَى مَغْفِرَةٍ مِنَ اللهِ وَرِضْوَانٍ ، قَالَ : فَتَخْرُجُ تَسِيلُ كَمَا تَسِيلُ الْقَطْرَةُ مِنْ فِي السِّقَاءِ . قَالَ : فَيَأْخُذُهَا ، فَإِذَا

---

[12] Reported by Muslim, number: 920.

أَخَذَهَا لَمْ يَدَعُوهَا فِي يَدِهِ طَرْفَةَ عَيْنٍ ، حَتَّى يَأْخُذُوهَا فَيَجْعَلُوهَا فِي ذَلِكَ الْكَفَنِ وَفِي ذَلِكَ الْحَنُوطِ ، وَيَخْرُجُ مِنْهَا كَأَطْيَبِ نَفْحَةِ مِسْكٍ وُجِدَتْ عَلَى وَجْهِ الأَرْضِ ، فَيَصْعَدُونَ بِهَا ، فَلا يَمُرُّونَ بِهَا عَلَى مَلإٍ مِنَ الْمَلائِكَةِ إِلا قَالُوا : مَا هَذِهِ الرُّوحُ الطَّيِّبَةُ ؟ قَالَ : فَيَقُولُونَ : فُلانُ بْنُ فُلانٍ ، بِأَحْسَنِ أَسْمَائِهِ الَّتِي كَانُوا يُسَمُّونَهُ فِي الدُّنْيَا ، حَتَّى يَنْتَهُونَ بِهَا إِلَى السَّمَاءِ الدُّنْيَا فَيَسْتَفْتِحُونَ لَهُ فَيُفْتَحُ لَهُ ، فَيُشَيِّعُهُ مِنْ كُلِّ سَمَاءٍ مُقَرَّبُوهَا إِلَى السَّمَاءِ الَّتِي تَلِيهَا ، حَتَّى يُنْتَهَى بِهَا إِلَى السَّمَاءِ السَّابِعَةِ . فَيَقُولُ اللهُ ، تَبَارَكَ وَتَعَالَى : اكْتُبُوا كِتَابَ عَبْدِي فِي عِلِّيِّينَ ، وَأَعِيدُوهُ إِلَى الأَرْضِ فَإِنَّا مِنْهَا خَلَقْنَاهُمْ وَفِيهَا أُعِيدُهُمْ وَمِنْهَا أُخْرِجُهُمْ تَارَةً أُخْرَى . فَقَالَ : فَيُعَادُ رُوحُهُ فِي جَسَدِهِ ، وَيَأْتِيهِ مَلَكَانِ فَيُجْلِسَانِهِ فَيَقُولانِ لَهُ : مَنْ رَبُّكَ ؟ فَيَقُولُ : رَبِّيَ اللهُ ، فَيَقُولانِ : مَا دِينُكَ ؟ فَيَقُولُ : دِينِي الإِسْلامُ ، فَيَقُولانِ لَهُ : مَا هَذَا الرَّجُلُ الَّذِي بُعِثَ فِيكُمْ ؟ فَيَقُولُ : هُوَ رَسُولُ اللهِ ، صَلَّى اللهُ عَلَيْهِ وَسَلَّمَ ، فَيَقُولانِ : وَمَا عِلْمُكَ ؟ فَيَقُولُ : قَرَأْتُ كِتَابَ اللهِ ، عَزَّ وَجَلَّ ، فَآمَنْتُ بِهِ وَصَدَّقْتُهُ . قَالَ : فَيُنَادِي

مُنَادٍ مِنَ السَّمَاءِ أَنْ صَدَقَ عَبْدِي . فَأَفْرِشُوهُ مِنَ الْجَنَّةِ ، وَأَلْبِسُوهُ مِنَ الْجَنَّةِ ، وَافْتَحُوا لَهُ بَابًا إِلَى الْجَنَّةِ . قَالَ : فَيَأْتِيهِ مِنْ رُوحِهَا وَمِنْ طِيبِهَا . قَالَ : وَيُفْسَحُ لَهُ فِي قَبْرِهِ مَدَّ بَصَرِهِ ، وَيَأْتِيهِ رَجُلٌ حَسَنُ الْوَجْهِ حَسَنُ الثِّيَابِ طَيِّبُ الرِّيحِ ، فَيَقُولُ : أَبْشِرْ بِالَّذِي يَسُرُّكَ ، هَذَا الَّذِي كُنْتَ تُوعَدُ . فَيَقُولُ : مَنْ أَنْتَ ؟ فَوَجْهُكَ الْوَجْهُ يَجِيءُ بِالْخَيْرِ . فَيَقُولُ : أَنَا عَمَلُكَ الصَّالِحُ . قَالَ : فَيَقُولُ : رَبِّ ، أَقِمِ السَّاعَةَ حَتَّى أَرْجِعَ إِلَى أَهْلِي وَمَالِي . وَإِنَّ الْعَبْدَ الْكَافِرَ إِذَا كَانَ فِي انْقِطَاعٍ مِنَ الدُّنْيَا ، وَإِقْبَالٍ مِنَ الآخِرَةِ ؛ نَزَلَ إِلَيْهِ مَلائِكَةٌ سُودُ الْوَجْهِ مَعَهُمُ الْمُسُوحُ . قَالَ : فَيَجْلِسُونَ مِنْهُ مَدَّ الْبَصَرِ ، ثُمَّ يَجِيءُ مَلَكُ الْمَوْتِ ، صَلَّى اللهُ عَلَيْهِ وَسَلَّمَ ، حَتَّى يَجْلِسَ عِنْدَ رَأْسِهِ ، فَيَقُولُ : أَيَّتُهَا النَّفْسُ الْخَبِيثَةُ ، اخْرُجِي إِلَى سَخَطِ اللهِ وَغَضَبِهِ . قَالَ : فَتَنْطَوِي فِي جَسَدِهِ . قَالَ : فَيَنْتَزِعُهَا كَمَا يُنْتَزَعُ السَّفُّودُ مِنَ الصُّوفِ الْمَبْلُولِ . فَتُقْطَعُ مِنْهَا الْعُرُوقُ وَالْعَصَبُ . قَالَ : فَيَأْخُذُهَا ، فَإِذَا أَخَذَهَا ؛ لَمْ يَدَعُوهَا فِي يَدِهِ طَرْفَةَ عَيْنٍ حَتَّى يَأْخُذُونَهَا ، فَيَجْعَلُونَهَا فِي تِلْكَ الْمُسُوحِ ، فَيَخْرُجُ مِنْهَا كَأَنْتَنِ رِيحِ جِيفَةٍ وُجِدَتْ عَلَى الأَرْضِ . قَالَ :

فَيَصْعَدُونَ بِهَا فَلا يَمُرُّونَ بِمَلإٍ مِنَ الْمَلائِكَةِ إِلا قَالُوا : مَا هَذِهِ الرُّوحُ الْخَبِيثَةُ ؟ قَالَ : ((فَيَقُولُونَ : فُلانُ بْنُ فُلانٍ ، بِأَقْبَحِ أَسْمَائِهِ الَّتِي كَانَ يُسَمَّى بِهَا فِي الدُّنْيَا ، حَتَّى يُنْتَهَى بِهَا إِلَى السَّمَاءِ الدُّنْيَا ، فَيُسْتَفْتَحُ لَهُ فَلا يُفْتَحُ لَهُ)) . ثُمَّ قَرَأَ رَسُولُ اللهِ ، صَلَّى اللهُ عَلَيْهِ وَسَلَّمَ ، لا تُفَتَّحُ لَهُمْ أَبْوَابُ السَّمَاءِ وَلا يَدْخُلُونَ الْجَنَّةَ حَتَّى يَلِجَ الْجَمَلُ فِي سَمِّ الْخِيَاطِ سورة الأعراف آية ٤٠ . قَالَ :((فَيَقُولُ اللهُ، عَزَّ وَجَلَّ : اكْتُبُوا كِتَابَهُ فِي سِجِّينٍ فِي الأَرْضِ السُّفْلَى ، قَالَ : فَيُطْرَحُ عَلَى وَجْهِهِ طَرْحًا)) . ثُمَّ قَرَأَ رَسُولُ اللهِ ، صَلَّى اللهُ عَلَيْهِ وَسَلَّمَ : وَمَنْ يُشْرِكْ بِاللهِ فَكَأَنَّمَا خَرَّ مِنَ السَّمَاءِ فَتَخْطَفُهُ الطَّيْرُ أَوْ تَهْوِي بِهِ الرِّيحُ فِي مَكَانٍ سَحِيقٍ سورة الحج آية ٣١ . قَالَ : ((فَيُعَادُ رُوحُهُ فِي جَسَدِهِ ، وَيَأْتِيهِ مَلَكَانِ فَيُجْلِسَانِهِ فَيَقُولانِ لَهُ : مَنْ رَبُّكَ ؟ فَيَقُولُ : هَاهْ هَاهْ لا أَدْرِي ، فَيَقُولانِ لَهُ : مَا دِينُكَ ؟ فَيَقُولُ : هَاهْ هَاهْ لا أَدْرِي ، فَيَقُولانِ لَهُ : مَا هَذَا الرَّجُلُ الَّذِي بُعِثَ فِيكُمْ ؟ فَيَقُولُ : هَاهْ هَاهْ لا أَدْرِي . فَيُنَادِي مُنَادٍ مِنَ السَّمَاءِ أَنْ كَذَبَ . فَأَفْرِشُوهُ مِنَ النَّارِ ، وَأَلْبِسُوهُ مِنَ النَّارِ ، وَافْتَحُوا لَهُ بَابًا مِنَ

النَّارِ ، قَالَ : فَيَأْتِيهِ مِنْ حَرِّهَا وَسَمُومِهَا ، قَالَ : وَيُضَيَّقُ عَلَيْهِ قَبْرُهُ حَتَّى تَخْتَلِفَ فِي أَضْلاعِهِ ، وَيَأْتِيهِ رَجُلٌ قَبِيحُ الْوَجْهِ قَبِيحُ الثِّيَابِ مُنْتَنُ الرِّيحِ ، فَيَقُولُ : أَبْشِرْ بِالَّذِي يَسُوءُكَ ، هَذَا يَوْمُكَ الَّذِي كُنْتَ تُوعَدُ . فَيَقُولُ : مَنْ أَنْتَ ، فَوَجْهُكَ الْوَجْهُ يَجِيءُ بِالشَّرِّ ؟ فَيَقُولُ : أَنَا عَمَلُكَ الْخَبِيثُ ، فَيَقُولُ : رَبِّ ، لا تُقِمِ السَّاعَةَ ، رَبِّ لا تُقِمِ السَّاعَةَ

"We went out with the Prophet (sallallahu alaihi wa sallam) to the burial of a man from the Ansar until we arrived at the grave, and he still had not been placed in the grave. Then the Messenger of Allah (sallallahu alaihi wa sallam) sat down facing the Qiblah and we sat around him. You would have thought that birds were upon our heads from our silence, and in the hand of the Messenger of Allah (sallallahu alaihi wa sallam) was a stick which he was poking the ground with. Then he started looking at the sky and looking at the earth and then he looked up and down three times. Then he said to us: 'Ask Allah for refuge from the torment of the grave.' He repeated this command two or three times. Then he said: 'Oh Allah, I seek refuge in you from the torment of the grave,' three times. Then he said: 'Verily, the believing slave, when leaving this life and heading to the hereafter, angels will descend upon him; their faces will be white as if they were suns; they will have with them a shroud from the

shrouds of Paradise, and an embalmment from the embalmment's of heaven. Then, they will sit within eye-shot of him. Then the angel of death (alaihi assalaam) will come and sit at his head and will say 'Oh you virtuous (and in another narration: peaceful) soul, come out to a forgiveness and a pleasure from your Lord.' So it will come out as a drop comes out of the mouth of a jug, then he will take it (or in another narration: until the soul comes out and every angel between the heavens and the earth and every angel in the heavens prays for him, and the heavens' gates are opened, and there is not an inhabitant of the gates except that they are calling to Allah to be the one that the soul is risen to), not leaving it in his hand for longer than a blink of an eye until they have placed it in that shroud and that embalmment. And that is the meaning of His, the Most High's, saying: 'Our Messengers take his soul, and they never neglect their duty.'[13] And there will emanate from him a smell like that of the sweetest smelling musk on the face of the earth.

"Then they shall ascend with it (the soul) and they shall not pass with it by any group of angels except that they will say: 'What is this good and sweet-smelling soul?' Then they shall say to them: 'So and so, son of so and so,' choosing the best of the names he used to be called by in this life. They ascend until they reach the lowest sky; then they shall ask permission to enter, and they shall be granted entry, and they proceed to each heaven until they end at

[13] Soorah Al-An'am (6: 61)

the seventh heaven; then Allah, Exalted and High, shall say:

"'Write the book of my servant in the *Illiyyeen*.' And what will make you know what *Illiyyun* is? A register inscribed. To which bear witness those nearest (to Allah, i.e., the angels).'[14]

"So his book will be written in the *lliyyeen*, and it shall be said: 'Return him to the earth, for I promised them I have created them from it, and into it, I shall return them, and from it, I shall resurrect them once again.'

"He said: 'So he is returned to earth and his soul is returned to his body.' He said: 'And he will hear the footsteps of his friends as they leave him. Then two angels, severe in their reproachment, shall come and terrify him and sit him up and shall ask him: 'Who is your Lord?' He shall reply: 'My Lord is Allah.' Then they shall ask him: 'What is your religion?' He shall answer them: 'My religion is Islam.' Then they shall ask him: 'Who is this man who was sent among you?' He will reply: 'He is the Messenger of Allah (sallallahu alaihi wa sallam).' Then they shall ask him: 'What have you done?' He shall reply: 'I read the book of Allah, then I believed in it and accepted it.' Then the angel will terrify him and ask him: 'Who is your Lord? What is your religion? Who is your prophet?' and this will be the last trial on earth

---

[14] Soorah Al-Mutaffifin (83: 18)

for the believer. It is then when Allah, the Almighty, the Venerable, says:

"'Allah will keep firm those who believe, with the word that stands firm in this world.'[15]

"So he will answer: 'My Lord is Allah, my religion is Islam and my Prophet is Muhammad (sallallahu alaihi wa sallam).' Then a caller will call from the sky: 'My slave has spoken the truth, so spread out for him from heaven, and clothe him from heaven, and open a door for him from heaven.' He said: 'So its goodness and its smell will come unto him and his grave will be expanded for him as far as he can see.'

"Then a man will come to him (and in another narration: will be embodied for him). His face will be handsome, his clothes will be nice, and his smell will be sweet. Then he shall say unto him: 'I bring you glad tidings of that which will make you happy: rejoice with Allah's pleasure and gardens in which there is enduring bliss. This is the day that you were promised.' Then he will say: 'May Allah give you glad tidings of goodness; who are you, for your face is the face of someone who comes with good news?' He shall reply: 'I am your good deeds, by Allah, I did not know you but that you were quick to the obedience of Allah and slow to His disobedience, so may Allah reward you with good.' "Then a door to Heaven and Hell is opened for him and it is said to

---

[15] Soorah Ibrahim (14: 27)

him: 'This is your place; if you had disobeyed Allah, He would have replaced it with this.' When he saw that which is in Heaven he said: 'My Lord, bring the hour so that I might return to my family and my wealth.' It will be said to him 'Be calm.'

"He said: 'And the disbelieving (and in another narration: wicked) slave, when leaving this life and heading to the hereafter, then rough, severe angels will descend upon him, their faces will be black, they will have with them a sack made of fire. Then they will sit within eye-shot of him. Then the angel of death will come and sit at his head and will say: 'Oh you wicked soul; come out to your Lord's anger and fury."

"He said: 'So it will spread out throughout his body, then he will rip it out as a skewer with many prongs is ripped out of damp cotton and it tears and cuts the nerves and blood vessels as it is removed. Then he will be cursed by all the angels between the heavens and the earth and by all the angels in the heavens, and the gates of heaven are closed. There is not an inhabitant of the gates except that they are calling to Allah that the wicked soul is not ascended to their side. Then he will take it, not leaving it in his hand for longer than a blink of an eye until they have placed it in that sack. And there will emanate from it a stench like that of the most foul smelling corpse on the face of the earth. Then they shall ascend with it, and they shall not pass with it by a group of angels except they will say: 'Who is this wicked soul?' Then they shall say to them: 'Such and such, son of such and such,' choosing the most hated of the names he used to be called in this life. When they reach the lowest heaven they shall ask permission to enter, and they shall not be granted entry." Then the Messenger of Allah (sallallahu alaihi wa sallam) recited: "For them, the gates of heaven will not be opened, and they will not enter Paradise until the camel goes through the eye of the needle.'[16]

"Then Allah, Almighty and Venerable, shall say: 'Write his book in the *Sijjeen* in the lowest earth.' Then it will be said: 'Return my slave to the earth, for I promised them that I have created them from it, and into it, I shall return them, and from it, I shall resurrect them once again.'

"Then his soul shall be thrown from the sky with a mighty hurl until it is cast into his body.' Then he (the Prophet sallallahu alaihi wa sallam) read: "And whoever assigns partners to Allah, it is as if he had fallen from the sky, and the birds had snatched him, or the wind had thrown him to a far off place.'[17] Then his soul will be returned to his body.'

"He (the prophet) said: 'Verily, he will hear the footsteps of his friends when they leave him. Then two harsh, severe and fearsome angels shall come and terrify him and sit him up and they shall ask him: 'Who is your Lord?' He shall reply: 'Huh? Huh? I do not know.' Then they shall ask him: 'What is

---

[16] Soorah Al-A'raf (7: 40)
[17] Soorah Al-Hajj (22: 31)

your religion?' He shall answer them: 'Huh? Huh? I do not know.' Then they shall ask him: 'Who is this man who was sent among you?' He was not guided to his name so it was said: 'Muhammad! Then he said: Huh? Huh? I do not know; I heard people saying that!'

"He (the Prophet sallallahu alaihi wa sallam) said: 'And then it will be said to him: 'Neither do you know nor did you recite!' Then a caller will call from the sky: 'He disbelieved! So spread out for him to the hell fire, and open a door for him to the hell fire!' So, its heat and hot wind will come unto him, and his grave will become narrow until his limbs are caught up among one another.

"Then a man will come to him (or in another narration: will be embodied for him). His face will be ugly, and his clothes will be ugly, and his smell will be vile. Then he shall say to him: 'I bring you tidings of that which will harm you. This is the day that you were promised.' Then he will say: 'And you, may Allah give you tidings of evil! Who are you? Your face is the face of someone who brings evil.' He shall reply: 'I am your evil deeds, by Allah, I did not know of you except that you were quick to the disobedience of Allah and slow to His obedience, so, may Allah recompense you with bad!' Then there will be assigned to him a blind, deaf and mute person who holds in his hand a hammer' if a mountain were hit with it, it would disintegrate, and he will beat him with it until he becomes dust, and then Allah will render him to his initial form, and

he will beat him again, and he will scream out with a cry that will be heard by everything except humans and jinn, and a door of hell will be opened unto him within his grave and will spread out for him sheets of hell fire.' Then he shall say: 'My Lord, do not bring the hour.'[18]

8. It is related from Awf bin Malik (radiallahu anhu) that he said:

صَلَّى رَسُولُ اللهِ - صَلَّى اللهُ عَلَيْهِ وَ سَلَّمَ - عَلَى جَنَازَةٍ ، فَحَفِظْتُ مِنْ دُعَائِهِ وَ هُوَ يَقُولُ : ((اَللَّهُمَّ اغْفِرْ لَهُ ، وَارْحَمْهُ ، وَ عَافِهِ ، وَاعْفُ عَنْهُ ، وَ أَكْرِمْ نُزُلَهُ ، وَ وَسِّعْ مُدْخَلَهُ ، وَاغْسِلْهُ بِالْمَاءِ وَ الثَّلْجِ وَ الْبَرَدِ ، وَ نَقِّهِ مِنَ الْخَطَايَا كَمَا يُنَقَّى الثَّوْبُ الْأَبْيَضُ مِنَ الدَّنَسِ ، وَ أَبْدِلْهُ دَارًا خَيْرًا مِنْ دَارِهِ ، وَ أَهْلًا خَيْرًا مِنْ أَهْلِهِ ، وَزَوْجًا خَيْرًا مِنْ زَوْجِهِ ، وَ أَدْخِلْهُ الْجَنَّةَ ،

---

[18] Reported by At-Tayalasi, number: 752; Ahmad, number: 30/499; Al-Hakim, number: 1/37-40; Abu Dawud, number: 4753; and Al-Ajurry in "Ash-Shari'ah." Abu Na'im declared it to be authentic, as well as Al-Hakim, Adh-Dhahabi, Ibn Al-Qayyim in "Ahkam Al-Jana'iz", pages: 189-202, the Al-Ma'arif Publications print.
Sheikh Muqbil declared it as good in "As-Sahih Al-Musnad Mimma Laisa fi As-Sahihain".

وَ أَعِذْهُ مِنْ عَذَابِ الْقَبْرِ ، وَ مِنْ عَذَابِ النَّارِ)) . قَالَ :
فَتَمَنَّيْتُ أَنْ أَكُونَ أَنَا ذَلِكَ الْمَيِّتَ .

"The Messenger of Allah prayed over the deceased so I memorized his supplication, he said: 'Oh Allah, forgive him, have mercy upon him, give him peace and absolve him. Receive him with honour and make his grave spacious; wash him with water, snow and hail. Cleanse him from faults as a white garment is cleansed from dirt. Replace him with an abode more excellent than his abode, with a family better than his family, and with a partner better than his partner. Admit him to the Garden, and protect him from the torment of the grave and the torment of the Fire.'" He said: "I wished that I were this dead body." [19]

9. It is related from Abi Hurayrah:

إِذَا خَرَجَتْ رُوحُ الْمُؤْمِنِ ، تَلَقَّاهَا مَلَكَانِ يُصْعِدَانِهَا
- قَالَ حَمَّادٌ : فَذَكَرَ مِنْ طِيبِ رِيحِهَا ، وَ ذَكَرَ
الْمِسْكَ - قَالَ : وَ يَقُولُ أَهْلُ السَّمَاءِ : رُوحٌ طَيِّبَةٌ
جَاءَتْ مِنْ قِبَلِ الْأَرْضِ ، صَلَّى اللهُ عَلَيْكِ ، وَ عَلَى

---

[19] Reported by Muslim, number: 963.
As it is reported in "Ahkam Al-Jana'iz" by Sheikh Al-Albani (rahimahullah), page: 157.

جَسَدٍ كُنْتِ تَعْمُرِينَهُ فَيُنْطَلَقُ بِهِ إِلَى رَبِّهِ عَزَّ وَ جَلَّ ، ثُمَّ يَقُولُ : انْطَلِقُوا بِهِ إِلَى آخِرِ الْأَجَلِ .

قَالَ : وَ إِنَّ الْكَافِرَ إِذَا خَرَجَتْ رُوحُهُ - قَالَ حَمَّادٌ : وَ ذَكَرَ مِنْ نَتْنِهَا ، وَ ذَكَرَ لَعْنًا - وَ يَقُولُ أَهْلُ السَّمَاءِ : رُوحٌ خَبِيثَةٌ جَائَتْ مِنْ قِبَلِ الْأَرْضِ . قَالَ : فَيُقَالُ : انْطَلِقُوا بِهِ إِلَى آخِرِ الْأَجَلِ .

قَالَ أَبُو هُرَيْرَةَ رَضِيَ اللهُ عَنْهُ : فَرَدَّ رَسُولُ اللهِ - صَلَّى اللهُ عَلَيْهِ وَ سَلَّمَ - رَيْطَةً كَانَتْ عَلَيْهِ ، عَلَى أَنْفِهِ ، هَكَذَا .

"When the soul of a believer exits (the body), it is received by two angels who raise it up." Hammad mentioned the sweetness of its scent and he mentioned the musk. The inhabitants of the heavens said: "Here comes the pious soul from earth, may Allah bless you and the body in which you used to reside." It is carried to its Lord, the Exalted and Glorious. Then he says: "Take it to its last."

When the disbeliever's soul leaves the body, Hammad made a mention of its foul smell and of its being cursed, the inhabitants of the heavens say: "A dirty soul from earth." He said: "And it is said: 'Take it to its last appointment.'"

Abu Hurayrah (radiallahu anhu) said: "The Messenger of Allah (sallallahu alaihi wa sallam) put a thin cloth which was with him upon his nose like this." [20]

10. It is related from Masruq that he said:

سَأَلْنَا عَبْدَاللهِ بْنِ مَسْعُودٍ عَنْ هَذِهِ الْآيَةِ : ﴿ وَلَا تَحْسَبَنَّ ٱلَّذِينَ قُتِلُوا۟ فِى سَبِيلِ ٱللَّهِ أَمْوَٰتًۢا ۚ بَلْ أَحْيَآءٌ عِندَ رَبِّهِمْ يُرْزَقُونَ ﴿١٦٩﴾ ﴾ قَالَ : أَمَا إِنَّا قَدْ سَأَلْنَا عَنْ ذَلِكَ ، فَقَالَ : إِنَّ أَرْوَاحَ الشُّهَدَاءِ فِي جَوْفِ طَيْرٍ خُضْرٍ ، لَهَا قَنَادِيلُ مُعَلَّقَةٌ تَحْتَ الْعَرْشِ ، تَسْرَحُ مِنَ الْجَنَّةِ حَيْثُ شَاءَتْ ، ثُمَّ تَأْوِي إِلَى تِلْكَ الْقَنَادِيلِ ، فَاطَّلَعَ إِلَيْهِمْ رَبُّهُمْ اطِّلَاعَةً ، فَقَالَ : هَلْ تَشْتَهُونَ شَيْئًا ؟ قَالُوا : أَيَّ شَيْءٍ نَشْتَهِي ، وَ نَحْنُ نَسْرَحُ مِنَ الْجَنَّةِ حَيْثُ شِئْنَا ؟ فَيَفْعَلُ ذَلِكَ بِهِمْ ثَلَاثَ مَرَّاتٍ ، فَلَمَّا رَأَوْا أَنَّهُمْ لَمْ يُتْرَكُوا مِنْ يُسْأَلُوا ، قَالُوا : يَا رَبِّ ! نُرِيدُ أَنْ تَرُدَّ أَرْوَاحَنَا فِي أَجْسَادِنَا ، حَتَّى نَرْجِعَ إِلَى الدُّنْيَا ، فَنُقْتَلَ فِي سَبِيلِكَ مَرَّةً أُخْرَى . فَلَمَّا رَأَى أَنْ لَيْسَ لَهُمْ حَاجَةٌ تُرِكُوا .

[20] Reported by Muslim on his own, number: 2872.

"We asked Abdullah bin Mas'ud about this verse: 'Think not of those who are killed in the way of Allah as dead. Nay, they are alive, with their Lord, and they have provision.'"[21]

"He said: 'We asked about the verse (from the Prophet) and he said: 'The souls, of the martyrs live in the bodies of green birds who have their nests in chandeliers hung from the throne of the Almighty. They eat the fruits of Paradise from wherever they like and then nestle in these chandeliers. Their Lord cast a glance at them and said: 'Do you desire anything?' They said: 'What more can we desire? We eat the fruit of Paradise from wherever we like.' Their Lord asked them the same question three times. When they saw that they will continue to be asked and not left, they said: 'Oh Lord, we wish that you may return our souls to our bodies, so that we may return to the Dunya and be slain in your cause once again.' When He saw that they had no need, they were left.''" [22]

---

[21] Soorah Aal-Imran (3: 169)

[22] Reported by Imam Muslim, number: 1887; and At-Tirmidhi.
At-Tirmidhi reported it on the authority of Ka'b bin Malik, as it is in Sahih Al-Jami' by Sheikh Al-Albani (rahimahullah), number: 1559.
Ibn Majah reported on the authority Umm Bashr bin Al-Bara bin Ma'rur and Ka'b bin Malik, as it is in "Sahih Al-Jami'" by Sheikh Al-Albani (rahimahullah), number: 1560.

A Summary Of The Pleasures Of The Grave

1. Its width.

2. Its comfort.

3. The grave of the believer is lit like the night of a full moon.

4. The opening of a door to Heaven.

5. The opening of a window to Heaven.

6. The believer's clothes in the grave.

7. His righteous companions.

8. His surety at the time of questioning.

9. His request to the angels to be allowed to pray.

10. His request to be returned to his family to give them glad tidings.

11. The believer's supplication to his Lord whilst in the grave: "Oh Lord, establish the hour."

12. The believer's saying to his pallbearers: "Bring me forth, bring me forth."

13. The angels' glad tidings of the Lord's pleasure and Heaven for the believer when he is brought near.

14. The believer's love for meeting his Lord when he approaches it.

15. The believers' happiness to meet Him, sit with Him, and being spoken to.

16. The angels that come with the angel of death to remove the soul have white faces.

17. The believer's soul is wrapped in a shroud and embalmment from Heaven by the angels.

18. The believer's soul is raised up to the seventh heaven.

19. And he is followed by those that are near to each heaven.

20. He is mentioned in the heavens by the most beloved names to him.

21. His soul emanates the scent of the most beautiful perfume.

22. There is not a single guardian of the gates of the heavens except that they ask Allah to raise him by way of them.

23. Allah's saying to the angels: "Write my slave's book in the *Illiyeen*."

24. The angels saying to the believer: "Sleep the sleep of the groom who does not awake except that his family has become more beloved to him."

25. The righteous companion's saying to the believer: "May Allah reward you with good, for by Allah, indeed, I knew you to rush to do good but you were slow to do evil."

26. The believer in his grave bears witness that there is none worthy of worship except Allah and that Muhammad is the messenger of Allah.

27. The believer is shown his place in Heaven day and night.

28. The saying of the inhabitants of the heavens to the souls of the believers: "A good soul has come from the people of Earth, may Allah bless you and your body that you used to inhabit."

29. The grave is a green garden for the believer.

30. The angels place the soul of the believer in white silk.

31. The believer is relaxed in his grave.

CHAPTER 3: THE PUNISHMENT OF THE GRAVE

11. It is related from Abu Ayub Al-Ansari (radiallahu anhu) that he said:

خَرَجَ النَّبِيُّ - صَلَّى اللهُ عَلَيْهِ وَ سَلَّمَ وَ قَدْ وَجَبَتْ الشَّمْسُ ، فَسَمِعَ صَوْتًا ، فَقَالَ : ((يَهُودُ تُعَذَّبُ فِي قُبُورِهَا)) .

"The Prophet (sallallahu alaihi wa sallam) went out when the sun had set and he heard a sound and said: 'A Jew being punished in the grave.'" [23]

12. It is related from 'A'isha that a Jewish woman came to her and mentioned the punishment of the grave saying:

أَعَاذَكِ اللهُ مِنْ عَذَابِ الْقَبْرِ . فَسَأَلَتْ عَائِشَةُ رَسُولَ اللهِ - صَلَّى اللهُ عَلَيْهِ وَ سَلَّمَ - عَنْ عَذَابِ الْقَبْرِ ، فَقَالَ : ((نَعَمْ ، عَذَابُ الْقَبْرِ حَقٌّ)) . قَالَتْ عَائِشَةُ - رَضِيَ اللهُ عَنْهَا - : فَمَا رَأَيْتُ رَسُولَ اللهِ - صَلَّى اللهُ عَلَيْهِ وَ سَلَّمَ - بَعْدُ صَلَّى صَلَاةً إِلَّا تَعَوَّذَ مِنْ عَذَابِ الْقَبْرِ .

---

[23] Reported by Al-Bukhari, number: 1309; and Muslim, number: 2869.

"May Allah give you refuge from the punishment of the grave!" So 'A'isha asked the Messenger of Allah (sallallahu alaihi wa sallam) about the punishment of the grave. He said: "Yes, the punishment of the grave exists." 'A'isha said: "After that, I never saw the Messenger of Allah (sallallahu alaihi wa sallam) pray a prayer without seeking refuge in Allah from the punishment of the grave."[24]

13. It is related from Abu Hurayrah that the Messenger of Allah (sallallahu alaihi wa sallam) passed by a grave and said:

ائْتُونِي بِجَرِيدَتَيْنِ)) فَجَعَلَ إِحْدَاهُمَا عِنْدَ رَأْسِهِ ، وَ الْأُخْرَى عِنْدَ رِجْلَيْهِ ، فَقِيلَ : يَا نَبِيَّ الله ! أَ يَنْفَعُهُ ذَلِكَ ؟ قَالَ : ((لَنْ يَزَالَ يُخَفَّفَ عَنْهُ بَعْضُ عَذَابِ الْقَبْرِ ، مَا كَانَ فِيهِمَا نُدُوٌّ)) .

"Bring me two palm stems." Then he put one at his head and the other at his feet, and it was said: "Oh Prophet of Allah, will this benefit him?" He said: "Some of the punishments of the grave will be relieved for as long as these remain moist." [25]

---

[24] Reported by Al-Bukhari, number: 1306; and Muslim, number: 903, 584, and 586. And see As-Silsalah As-Sahihah by Sheikh Al-Albani, number: 1377; and Sahih At-Targhib wat Tarhib, number: 3557.

[25] Reported by Ahmad: (15/429), (9686), checking done by Shu'aib and Ibn Abi Shaibah.

14. It is related that Anas bin Malik said:

أَخْبَرَنِي بَعْضُ مَنْ لَا أَتَّهِمُهُ مِنْ أَصْحَابِ النَّبِيِّ - صَلَّى اللهُ عَلَيْهِ وَ سَلَّمَ - أَنَّهُ قَالَ : بَيْنَمَا رَسُولُ اللهِ - صَلَّى اللهُ عَلَيْهِ وَ سَلَّمَ - وَ بِلَالٌ يَمْشِيَانِ بِالْبَقِيعِ ، فَقَالَ رَسُولُ اللهِ - صَلَّى اللهُ عَلَيْهِ وَ سَلَّمَ : ((يَا بِلَالُ ، هَلْ تَسْمَعُ مَا أَسْمَعُ ؟)) . قَالَ : لَا وَ اللهِ يَا رَسُولَ اللهِ مَا أَسْمَعُهُ . قَالَ : ((أَ لَا تَسْمَعُ أَهْلَ هَذِهِ الْقُبُورِ يَعَذَّبُونَ ؟)) . يَعْنِي : قُبُورَ الْجَاهِلِيَّةِ .

"Some of the companions of the Prophet (sallallahu alaihi wa sallam), in whom I have no doubt, informed me that one day the Messenger of Allah and Bilal were walking through Al-Baqee' when the Messenger of Allah said: 'Oh Bilal, do you hear what I'm hearing?' He said: 'No, by Allah, oh messenger of Allah.' He said: 'Do you not hear the people of these graves being punished?' Meaning, the graves of *Jahiliyah*." [26]

Sheikh Muqbil declared it to be authentic in "Jami' As-Sahih Mimma Laisa fis Sahihain": (2/278).

[26] Reported by Ahmad (21/271). Shuaib Al-Arna'ut declared it authentic in his checking of Al-Musnad with the number: 13719, and he said: "In Al-Baqee' is a mistake; what has been memorized in Bilal's story is what happened in a garden owned by Abu Talhah."

15. It is related from Anas bin Malik (radiallahu anhu) that the Prophet (sallallahu alaihi wa sallam) said:

لَوْ لَا أَ لَّا تَدَافَنُوا ، لَدَعَوْتُ اللهَ أَنْ يُسْمِعَكُمْ مِنْ عَذَابِ الْقَبْرِ .

"If it were not that you would cease to bury the dead in the graves, I would ask Allah to let you hear the punishment in the grave."[27]

16. It is related that Ibn 'Umar (radiallahu anhu) said that the Messenger of Allah (sallallahu alaihi wa sallam) said to his companions at Al-Hijr,

لَا تَدْخُلُوا عَلَى هَؤُلَاءِ الْمُعَذَّبِينَ ، إِلَّا أَنْ تَكُونُوا بَاكِينَ ، فَإِنْ لَمْ تَكُونُوا بَاكِينَ ، فَلَا تَدْخُلُوا عَلَيْهِمْ، لَا يُصِيبَكُمْ مَا أَصَابَهُمْ .

"Do not enter places of people who were punished unless you do so weeping. If you are not weeping then do not enter lest what befell them befalls you."[28]

[27] Reported by Imam Muslim alone, number: 2868.

[28] Reported by Al-Bukhari, number: 4157 and 423; and Muslim, number: 2980.

17. It is related that Jabir bin Abdullah Al-Ansari (radiallahu anhu) said that the Messenger of Allah (sallallahu alaihi wa sallam) said:

يَا جَابِرُ هَلْ رَأَيْتَ مَقَامِي ؟ قُلْتُ : نَعَمْ ، يَا رَسُولَ اللهِ . قَالَ : ((فَانْطَلِقْ إِلَى الشَّجَرَتَيْنِ ، فَاقْطَعْ مِنْ كُلِّ وَاحِدَةٍ مِنْهُمَا غُصْنًا عَنْ يَسَارِكَ)) . قَالَ جَابِرٌ : فَقُمْتُ ، فَأَخَذْتُ حَجَرًا ، فَكَسَرْتُهُ ، وَ حَسَرْتُهُ ، فَانْذَلَقَ لِي ، فَأَتَيْتُ الشَّجَرَتَيْنِ ، فَقَطَعْتُ مِنْ كُلِّ وَاحِدَةٍ مِنْهُمَا غُصْنًا ، ثُمَّ أَقْبَلْتُ أَجُرُّهُمَا ، حَتَّى قُمْتُ مَقَامَ رَسُولِ اللهِ - صَلَّى اللهُ عَلَيْهِ وَ سَلَّمَ - أَرْسَلْتُ غُصْنًا عَنْ يَمِينِي ، وَ غُصْنًا عَنْ يَسَارِي ، ثُمَّ لَحِقْتُهُ ، فَقُلْتُ : قَدْ فَعَلْتُ يَا رَسُولَ اللهِ ، فَعَمَّ ذَاكَ ؟ قَالَ : ((إِنِّي مَرَرْتُ بِقَبْرَيْنِ ، فَأَحْبَبْتُ بِشَفَاعَتِي أَنْ يُرَفَّهَ عَنْهُمَا ، مَا دَامَ الْغُصْنَانِ رَطْبَيْنِ)) .

"Jabir did you see where I was standing?" I said: "Yes, oh Messenger of Allah." He then said: "Then go to those two trees and cut a twig from each of them and take them to where I was standing and

stand there where I was standing and place a twig on the right and a twig on the left." Jabir said: "So I set out and took hold of a stone and broke it and sharpened it and then I came to those trees and cut a twig from each one of them. I then dragged them until I was stood at the place where the Messenger of Allah had stood and I placed a twig on the right and a twig on the left. Then I met him and said: 'Oh Messenger of Allah, I have done that, but please explain to me the reason for it.' So he said: 'I passed by two graves, the occupants of which were being tormented. I wanted to make intercession for them so that they may be relieved of this torment for as long as these twigs remain fresh.'"[29]

18. It is related that Abu Hurayrah said that a black woman (or a youth) used to sweep the masjid. The Messenger of Allah (sallallahu alaihi wa sallam) missed her and inquired about her (or him). The people told him that she he had died. He said:

أَ فَلَا كُنْتُمْ آذَنْتُمُونِي . قَالَ : فَكَأَنَّهُمْ صَغَّرُوا أَمْرَهَا.

(أَوْ أَمْرَهُ) ، فَقَالَ : ((دُلُّونِي عَلَى قَبْرِهِ)) فَدَلُّوهُ ،

فَصَلَّى عَلَيْهَا ، ثُمَّ قَالَ : ((إِنَّ هَذِهِ الْقُبُورَ مَمْلُوءَةٌ

[29] Reported by Al-Imam Muslim, number: 3012.

ظُلْمَةً عَلَى أَهْلِهَا ، وَ إِنَّ اللهَ عَزَّ وَ جَلَّ يُنَوِّرُهَا لَهُمْ بِصَلَاتِي عَلَيْهِمْ)) .

"Why did you not inform me?" It seemed as if they had belittled her situation (or his situation). He said: "Lead me to his grave." They led him there and he prayed over her and then said: "Verily, these graves are full of darkness for their dwellers. Verily, the Mighty and Glorious Allah illuminates them for their occupants, due to my prayer over them." [30]

19. It is related from Abdullah ibn Umar that the Messenger of Allah (sallallahu alaihi wa sallam) said:

إِنَّ أَحَدَكُمْ إِذَا مَاتَ ، عُرِضَ عَلَيْهِ مَقْعَدُهُ بِالْغَدَاةِ وَ الْعَشِيِّ ، فَإِنْ كَانَ مِنْ أَهْلِ الْجَنَّةِ ، فَمِنْ أَهْلِ الْجَنَّةِ ، وَ إِنْ كَانَ مِنْ أَهْلِ النَّارِ ، فَمِنْ أَهْلِ النَّارِ ، فَيُقَالُ : هَذَا مَقْعَدُكَ حَتَّى يَبْعَثَكَ اللهُ إِلَيْهِ يَوْمَ الْقِيَامَةِ)) .

"When one of you dies, he is shown his place morning and evening. If he is one of the people of the Heaven, then it is among the people of Heaven. If he is one of the people of the Fire, then it is among the people of the Fire. It is said: 'This is your

[30] Reported by Muslim, number: 956; and Baghawi (5/362).

place until Allah raises you up on the Day of Resurrection.'" [31]

[31] Reported by Al-Bukhari, number: 1313; and Muslim, number: 2866.

CHAPTER 4: REASONS FOR THE PUNISHMENT OF THE GRAVE

20. It is related from A'ishah, the wife of the Prophet (sallallahu alaihi wa sallam), that she said:

إِنَّمَا مَرَّ رَسُولُ اللهِ - صَلَّى اللهُ عَلَيْهِ وَ سَلَّمَ - عَلَى يَهُودِيَّةٍ ، يَبْكِي عَلَيْهَا أَهْلُهَا ، فَقَالَ : ((إِنَّهُمْ لَيَبْكُونَ عَلَيْهَا ، وَ إِنَّهَا لَتُعَذَّبُ فِي قَبْرِهَا))

"The Prophet (sallallahu alaihi wa sallam) passed by a Jewish woman whose family were crying for her, then he said: 'They are crying for her and she is being punished in her grave.'"[32]

21. It is related that Anas said,

كَانَ رَجُلٌ نَصْرَانِيًّا ، فَأَسْلَمَ ، وَ قَرَأَ الْبَقَرَةَ ، وَ آلَ عِمْرَانَ ، فَكَانَ يَكْتُبُ لِلنَّبِيِّ - صَلَّى اللهُ عَلَيْهِ وَ سَلَّمَ - ، فَعَادَ نَصْرَانِيًّا ، فَكَانَ يَقُولُ : مَا يَدْرِي مُحَمَّدٌ إِلَّا مَا كَتَبْتُ لَهُ . فَأَمَاتَهُ اللهُ ، فَدَفَنُوهُ ،

[32] Reported by Al-Bukhari, number: 1227; and Muslim, number: 932.

فَأَصْبَحَ وَ قَدْ لَفَظَتْهُ الْأَرْضُ ، فَقَالُوا : هَذَا فِعْلُ مَحَمَّدٍ وَ أَصْحَابِهِ ، لَمَّا هَرَبَ مِنْهُمْ نَبَشُوا عَنْ صَاحِبِنَا ، فَأَلْقَوْهُ. فَحَفَرُوا لَهُ ، فَأَعْمَقُوا ، فَأَصْبَحَ وَ قَدْ لَفَظَتْهُ الْأَرْضُ ، فَقَالُوا : هَذَا فِعْلُ مُحَمَّدٍ وَ أَصْحَابِهِ ، نَبَشُوا عَنْ صَاحِبِنَا ، لَمَّا هَرَبَ مِنْهُمْ ، فَأَلْقَوْهُ . فَحَفَرُوا لَهُ ، وَ أَعْمَقُوا لَهُ فِي الْأَرْضِ مَا اسْتَطَاعُوا ، فَأَصْبَحَ وَ قَدْ لَفَظَتْهُ الْأَرْضُ ، فَعَلِمُوا أَنَّهُ لَيْسَ مِنَ النَّاسِ ، فَأَلْقَوْهُ .

"There was a Christian man who became Muslim and recited Al-Baqara and Al-Imran. He used to act as a scribe for the Prophet (sallallahu alaihi wa sallam). Then he reverted to being a Christian and he used to say: 'Muhammad only knows what I wrote for him.' Allah caused him to die and they buried him. In the morning, the earth had thrown him up. They said: 'This is the work of Muhammad and his companions since he fled from them. They dug our companion up and threw him out.' So they dug a very deep grave and in the morning the earth had thrown him up. They said, 'This is the work of Muhammad and his companions since he fled from them. They dug our companion up and threw him out.' So they dug a grave for him as deep as they could and in the morning the earth had thrown him

up. So they knew that it was not done by people so they left him there."[33]

22. It is related that Ali said that on the day of (the Battle of) Al-Ahzab, the Messenger of Allah said:

مَلأَ اللهُ بُيُوتَهُمْ وَقُبُورَهُمْ نَارًا، شَغَلُونَا عَنِ الصَّلاةِ الْوُسْطَى حِينَ غَابَتِ الشَّمْسُ

"May Allah fill their homes and their graves with fire; they have distracted us from the middle prayer (i.e., Asr) until the sun set."[34]

23. It is related that Abdullah bin Mas'ood related that the Prophet (sallallahu alaihi wa sallam) said:

أُمِرَ بِعَبْدٍ مِنْ عِبَادِ اللهِ أَنْ يُضْرَبَ فِي قَبْرِهِ مَائَةَ جَلْدَةً ، فَلَمْ يَزَلْ يَسْأَلُ ، وَ يَدْعُو ، حَتَّى صَارَتْ جَلْدَةً وَاحِدَةً ، فَجُلِدَ جَلْدَةً وَاحِدَةً ، فَامْتَلأَ قَبْرُهُ عَلَيْهِ نَارًا ، فَلَمَّا ارْتَفَعَ عَنْهُ ، وَ أَفَاقَ ، قَالَ : عَلَى

---

[33] Reported by Al-Bukhari, number: 3421; and Muslim, number: 2781.
[34] Reported by Al-Bukhari, number: 2773; and Muslim, number: 627.

مَا جَلَدْتُمُونِي ؟ قَالُوا : إِنَّكَ صَلَّيْتَ صَلَاةً وَاحِدَةً بِغَيْرِ طَهُورٍ ، وَ مَرَرْتَ عَلَى مَظْلُومٍ فَلَمْ تَنْصُرْهُ .

"One of Allah's slaves was ordered to be beaten in his grave one hundred times. He never ceased asking and supplicating until it became one strike, so he was struck once and his grave became filled with fire. When he arose and regained consciousness he said: 'What did you strike me for?' They said: 'You prayed a prayer without purity and you passed someone that was oppressed without helping him.'"[35]

24. It is related that Anas bin Malik (radiallahu anhu) said:

لَمَّا عُرِجَ بِي مَرَرْتُ بِقَوْمٍ لَهُمْ أَظْفَارٌ مِنْ نُحَاسٍ يَخْمِشُونَ وُجُوهَهُمْ وَصُدُورَهُمْ فَقُلْتُ مَنْ هَؤُلَاءِ يَا جِبْرِيلُ قَالَ هَؤُلَاءِ الَّذِينَ يَأْكُلُونَ لُحُومَ النَّاسِ وَيَقَعُونَ فِي أَعْرَاضِهِمْ

"The Messenger of Allah (sallallahu alaihi wa sallam) said: 'When I was ascended, I passed a people whose nails were made of steel, with which they scratched at their faces and chests! So I

---

[35] Reported by At-Tahawi in "Mushkil Al-Aathar"
Sheikh Al-Albani (rahimahullah) declared its chain of narration to be "good" in "As-Silsilah As-Sahihah", number: 2774, and he said: "All of the narrators are trustworthy."

said: 'Who are they Jibril?' He said: 'They are the ones who eat the flesh, and speak about their honor.''"[36]

25. It is related that Samura ibn Jundub (radiallahu anhu) said:

كَانَ رَسُولُ اللَّهِ صلى الله عليه وسلم مِمَّا يُكْثِرُ أَنْ يَقُولَ لأَصْحَابِهِ " هَلْ رَأَى أَحَدٌ مِنْكُمْ مِنْ رُؤْيَا ". قَالَ فَيَقُصُّ عَلَيْهِ مَنْ شَاءَ اللهُ أَنْ يَقُصَّ، وَإِنَّهُ قَالَ ذَاتَ غَدَاةٍ " إِنَّهُ أَتَانِي اللَّيْلَةَ آتِيَانِ، وَإِنَّهُمَا ابْتَعَثَانِي، وَإِنَّهُمَا قَالاَ لِي انْطَلِقْ. وَإِنِّي انْطَلَقْتُ مَعَهُمَا، وَإِنَّا أَتَيْنَا عَلَى رَجُلٍ مُضْطَجِعٍ، وَإِذَا آخَرُ قَائِمٌ عَلَيْهِ بِصَخْرَةٍ، وَإِذَا هُوَ يَهْوِي بِالصَّخْرَةِ لِرَأْسِهِ، فَيَثْلَغُ رَأْسَهُ فَيَتَهَدْهَدُ الْحَجَرُ هَا هُنَا، فَيَتْبَعُ الْحَجَرَ فَيَأْخُذُهُ، فَلاَ يَرْجِعُ إِلَيْهِ حَتَّى يَصِحَّ رَأْسُهُ كَمَا كَانَ، ثُمَّ يَعُودُ عَلَيْهِ، فَيَفْعَلُ بِهِ مِثْلَ مَا فَعَلَ الْمَرَّةَ الأُولَى. قَالَ قُلْتُ لَهُمَا سُبْحَانَ اللهِ مَا هَذَانِ قَالَ قَالاَ لِي انْطَلِقْ ـ قَالَ ـ فَانْطَلَقْنَا فَأَتَيْنَا عَلَى رَجُلٍ

[36] Reported by Ahmad (3/224), and Abu Dawud, number: 4878. Al-Albani declared it authentic in Sahih Al-Jami', number: 5213, and in Sahih Sunan Abi Dawud, number 4082. See Silsilah As-Sahihah, number: 533.
Sheikh Muqbil Al-Wadi'i also declared it authentic in "As-Sahih Al-Musnad mimma Laisa fi As-Sahihain", number: (1/91).

مُسْتَلْقٍ لِقَفَاهُ، وَإِذَا آخَرُ قَائِمٌ عَلَيْهِ بِكَلُّوبٍ مِنْ حَدِيدٍ، وَإِذَا هُوَ يَأْتِي أَحَدَ شِقَّيْ وَجْهِهِ فَيُشَرْشِرُ شِدْقَهُ إِلَى قَفَاهُ، وَمَنْخِرَهُ إِلَى قَفَاهُ وَعَيْنَهُ إِلَى قَفَاهُ ـ قَالَ وَرُبَّمَا قَالَ أَبُو رَجَاءٍ فَيَشُقُّ ـ قَالَ ثُمَّ يَتَحَوَّلُ إِلَى الْجَانِبِ الآخَرِ، فَيَفْعَلُ بِهِ مِثْلَ مَا فَعَلَ بِالْجَانِبِ الأَوَّلِ، فَمَا يَفْرُغُ مِنْ ذَلِكَ الْجَانِبِ حَتَّى يَصِحَّ ذَلِكَ الْجَانِبُ كَمَا كَانَ، ثُمَّ يَعُودُ عَلَيْهِ فَيَفْعَلُ مِثْلَ مَا فَعَلَ الْمَرَّةَ الأُولَى. قَالَ قُلْتُ سُبْحَانَ اللهِ مَا هَذَانِ قَالَ قَالاَ لِي انْطَلِقْ. فَانْطَلَقْنَا فَأَتَيْنَا عَلَى مِثْلِ التَّنُّورِ ـ قَالَ فَأَحْسِبُ أَنَّهُ كَانَ يَقُولُ ـ فَإِذَا فِيهِ لَغَطٌ وَأَصْوَاتٌ ـ قَالَ ـ فَاطَّلَعْنَا فِيهِ، فَإِذَا فِيهِ رِجَالٌ وَنِسَاءٌ عُرَاةٌ، وَإِذَا هُمْ يَأْتِيهِمْ لَهَبٌ مِنْ أَسْفَلَ مِنْهُمْ، فَإِذَا أَتَاهُمْ ذَلِكَ اللَّهَبُ ضَوْضَوْا ـ قَالَ ـ قُلْتُ لَهُمَا مَا هَؤُلاَءِ قَالَ قَالاَ لِي انْطَلِقِ انْطَلِقْ. قَالَ فَانْطَلَقْنَا فَأَتَيْنَا عَلَى نَهَرٍ ـ حَسِبْتُ أَنَّهُ كَانَ يَقُولُ ـ أَحْمَرَ مِثْلِ الدَّمِ، وَإِذَا فِي النَّهَرِ رَجُلٌ سَابِحٌ يَسْبَحُ، وَإِذَا عَلَى شَطِّ النَّهَرِ رَجُلٌ قَدْ جَمَعَ عِنْدَهُ حِجَارَةً كَثِيرَةً، وَإِذَا ذَلِكَ السَّابِحُ يَسْبَحُ مَا يَسْبَحُ، ثُمَّ يَأْتِي ذَلِكَ الَّذِي قَدْ جَمَعَ عِنْدَهُ الْحِجَارَةَ فَيَفْغَرُ لَهُ فَاهُ فَيُلْقِمُهُ حَجَرًا فَيَنْطَلِقُ يَسْبَحُ، ثُمَّ يَرْجِعُ إِلَيْهِ، كُلَّمَا رَجَعَ إِلَيْهِ فَغَرَ لَهُ

فَاهُ فَأَلْقَمَهُ حَجَرًا ـ قَالَ ـ قُلْتُ لَهُمَا مَا هَذَانِ قَالَ قَالاَ لِي انْطَلِقِ انْطَلِقْ. قَالَ فَانْطَلَقْنَا فَأَتَيْنَا عَلَى رَجُلٍ كَرِيهِ الْمَرْآةِ كَأَكْرَهِ مَا أَنْتَ رَاءٍ رَجُلاً مَرْآةً، وَإِذَا عِنْدَهُ نَارٌ يَحُشُّهَا وَيَسْعَى حَوْلَهَا ـ قَالَ ـ قُلْتُ لَهُمَا مَا هَذَا قَالَ قَالاَ لِي انْطَلِقِ انْطَلِقْ. فَانْطَلَقْنَا فَأَتَيْنَا عَلَى رَوْضَةٍ مُعْتَمَّةٍ فِيهَا مِنْ كُلِّ نَوْرِ الرَّبِيعِ، وَإِذَا بَيْنَ ظَهْرَيِ الرَّوْضَةِ رَجُلٌ طَوِيلٌ لاَ أَكَادُ أَرَى رَأْسَهُ طُولاً فِي السَّمَاءِ، وَإِذَا حَوْلَ الرَّجُلِ مِنْ أَكْثَرِ وِلْدَانٍ رَأَيْتُهُمْ قَطُّ ـ قَالَ ـ قُلْتُ لَهُمَا مَا هَذَا مَا هَؤُلاَءِ قَالَ قَالاَ لِي انْطَلِقِ انْطَلِقْ. ـ قَالَ ـ فَانْطَلَقْنَا فَانْتَهَيْنَا إِلَى رَوْضَةٍ عَظِيمَةٍ لَمْ أَرَ رَوْضَةً قَطُّ أَعْظَمَ مِنْهَا وَلاَ أَحْسَنَ. ـ قَالَ ـ قَالاَ لِي ارْقَ فِيهَا. قَالَ فَارْتَقَيْنَا فِيهَا فَانْتَهَيْنَا إِلَى مَدِينَةٍ مَبْنِيَّةٍ بِلَبِنِ ذَهَبٍ وَلَبِنِ فِضَّةٍ، فَأَتَيْنَا باب الْمَدِينَةِ فَاسْتَفْتَحْنَا فَفُتِحَ لَنَا، فَدَخَلْنَاهَا فَتَلَقَّانَا فِيهَا رِجَالٌ شَطْرٌ مِنْ خَلْقِهِمْ كَأَحْسَنِ مَا أَنْتَ رَاءٍ، وَشَطْرٌ كَأَقْبَحِ مَا أَنْتَ رَاءٍ ـ قَالَ ـ قَالاَ لَهُمُ اذْهَبُوا فَقَعُوا فِي ذَلِكَ النَّهَرِ. قَالَ وَإِذَا نَهَرٌ مُعْتَرِضٌ يَجْرِي كَأَنَّ مَاءَهُ الْمَحْضُ فِي الْبَيَاضِ، فَذَهَبُوا فَوَقَعُوا فِيهِ، ثُمَّ رَجَعُوا إِلَيْنَا قَدْ ذَهَبَ ذَلِكَ السُّوءُ عَنْهُمْ، فَصَارُوا فِي أَحْسَنِ صُورَةٍ ـ قَالَ ـ

قَالاَ لِي هَذِهِ جَنَّةُ عَدْنٍ، وَهَذَاكَ مَنْزِلُكَ. قَالَ فَسَمَا بَصَرِي صُعُدًا، فَإِذَا قَصْرٌ مِثْلُ الرَّبَابَةِ الْبَيْضَاءِ ـ قَالَ ـ قَالاَ هَذَاكَ مَنْزِلُكَ. قَالَ قُلْتُ لَهُمَا بَارَكَ اللَّهُ فِيكُمَا، ذَرَانِي فَأَدْخُلَهُ. قَالاَ أَمَّا الآنَ فَلاَ وَأَنْتَ دَاخِلُهُ. قَالَ قُلْتُ لَهُمَا فَإِنِّي قَدْ رَأَيْتُ مُنْذُ اللَّيْلَةِ عَجَبًا، فَمَا هَذَا الَّذِي رَأَيْتُ قَالَ قَالاَ لِي أَمَا إِنَّا سَنُخْبِرُكَ، أَمَّا الرَّجُلُ الأَوَّلُ الَّذِي أَتَيْتَ عَلَيْهِ يُثْلَغُ رَأْسُهُ بِالْحَجَرِ، فَإِنَّهُ الرَّجُلُ يَأْخُذُ الْقُرْآنَ فَيَرْفُضُهُ وَيَنَامُ عَنِ الصَّلاَةِ الْمَكْتُوبَةِ، وَأَمَّا الرَّجُلُ الَّذِي أَتَيْتَ عَلَيْهِ يُشَرْشَرُ شِدْقُهُ إِلَى قَفَاهُ، وَمَنْخِرُهُ إِلَى قَفَاهُ، وَعَيْنُهُ إِلَى قَفَاهُ، فَإِنَّهُ الرَّجُلُ يَغْدُو مِنْ بَيْتِهِ فَيَكْذِبُ الْكَذْبَةَ تَبْلُغُ الآفَاقَ، وَأَمَّا الرِّجَالُ وَالنِّسَاءُ الْعُرَاةُ الَّذِينَ فِي مِثْلِ بِنَاءِ التَّنُّورِ فَإِنَّهُمُ الزُّنَاةُ وَالزَّوَانِي. وَأَمَّا الرَّجُلُ الَّذِي أَتَيْتَ عَلَيْهِ يَسْبَحُ فِي النَّهَرِ وَيُلْقَمُ الْحَجَرَ، فَإِنَّهُ آكِلُ الرِّبَا، وَأَمَّا الرَّجُلُ الْكَرِيهُ الْمَرْآةِ الَّذِي عِنْدَ النَّارِ يَحُشُّهَا وَيَسْعَى حَوْلَهَا، فَإِنَّهُ مَالِكٌ خَازِنُ جَهَنَّمَ، وَأَمَّا الرَّجُلُ الطَّوِيلُ الَّذِي فِي الرَّوْضَةِ فَإِنَّهُ إِبْرَاهِيمُ صلى الله عليه وسلم وَأَمَّا الْوِلْدَانُ الَّذِينَ حَوْلَهُ فَكُلُّ مَوْلُودٍ مَاتَ عَلَى الْفِطْرَةِ ". قَالَ فَقَالَ بَعْضُ الْمُسْلِمِينَ يَا رَسُولَ اللَّهِ

وَأَوْلاَدُ الْمُشْرِكِينَ فَقَالَ رَسُولُ اللهِ صلى اللهُ عليه وسلم :

((وَأَوْلاَدُ الْمُشْرِكِينَ. وَأَمَّا الْقَوْمُ الَّذِينَ كَانُوا شَطْرٌ مِنْهُمْ

حَسَنًا وَشَطَرٌ مِنْهُمْ قَبِيحًا، فَإِنَّهُمْ قَوْمٌ خَلَطُوا عَمَلاً صَالِحًا

وَآخَرَ سَيِّئًا، تَجَاوَزَ اللهُ عَنْهُمْ)).

"The Messenger of Allah (sallallahu alaihi wa sallam) used to frequently say: 'Has any of you had a dream?' Then whoever Allah wished would recount their dream. He said one morning: 'During the night, two men came to me and said to me, 'Come on!' So, I went with them. We came to a man who was lying on his back while another man was standing over him with a stone which he then dropped onto his head, crushing it. Then the stone rolled away from him and he went after the stone to retrieve it. When he returned to him, his head was whole again and had become as it had been in the first place. So he went back and hit him as he had done the first time. I said to them, 'Glory be to Allah! Who are these two?' They said, 'Go on! Go on!' We went on and came to a man who was lying on his back, and there was another man standing over him with an iron hook. He went to one side of his face and cut open the side of his mouth until it reached the back of his neck and then his nostril to the back of his neck and his eye to the back of his neck. (The narrator said perhaps Abu Rajaa said: *tear*.) Then he moved to the other side and did the same thing as he had done to the first side. When he finished that

side, the first side had become whole again. Then he did the same thing all over again. I said, 'Glory be to Allah! Who are these two?' They said to me, 'Go on! Go on!' And we went on until we came upon something like an oven. (I think he said: *There was babble and shouting in it.*) We looked down into it and it contained naked men and women. The flames would come at them from underneath, and when those flames reached them, they cried out. I asked, 'Who are they?' They said, 'Go on! Go on!' And we went on until we came to a river (I think that he said: *Red like blood*). In the river, there was a man swimming, while on the bank of the river, there was a man who had many stones with him. When that swimmer swam and reached the one who had gathered the stones, he forced his mouth open and made him swallow a stone. Then he would begin to swim and would come back to him again. Whenever he came back to him, he forced open his mouth and made him swallow a stone. I asked them: 'Who are these two?' They said to me, 'Go on! Go on!' And we went on until we came to a man with a repulsive appearance (or the most repulsive man you have ever seen). He was at a fire which he was kindling and which he was running around. I said to them: 'Who is this?' They said to me, 'Go on! Go on!' And we went on until we came to a green meadow containing every type of spring flower. In the middle of the meadow, there was a man so tall that I could scarcely see his head, so high it was in the sky. Around the man were the greatest number of children I have ever seen. I asked: 'Who is this? Who are they?' They told me: 'Go on! Go on!' And we went on until we reached a huge tree, and I have never seen any tree bigger or more beautiful than it. They told me: 'Climb it.' We climbed it and came to a city built of gold and silver bricks. We came to the door of the city and asked for it to be opened and it was opened for us and we entered it. We were met by men, half of whose physique was the most beautiful you have ever seen and the other half was the ugliest you have ever seen. The two said to them, 'Go and plunge into that river.' There was a wide river flowing there whose water was pure white. They went and jumped into it and when they returned to us, that evil had left them and they had the most beautiful form.'

"He said, 'They said to me: 'This is the everlasting paradise, and that is your place." I raised my eyes upwards and there was a castle like a white cloud. They said to me: 'This is your place.' I said to them: 'May Allah bless you; let me enter it.' They said: 'No, not now. But you will enter it.' I said to them: 'This night I have seen marvels, but what are these things which I have seen?' They said to me: 'We will tell you. The first man to whom you came whose head was being crushed with the stone is a man who memorized the Qur'an and then abandoned it and slept through the obligatory prayers. As for the man you came to whose jaw was split to his neck, whose nostril to his neck and whose eye to his neck, he was a man who went from

his house and told lies which spread everywhere. As for the naked men and women who were in something like an oven, they were adulterers and adulteresses. The man you came to who was swimming in the river and being made to swallow stones used to consume usury. The man with the disagreeable appearance who was at the fire, kindling it and running around it was Malik, the guardian of Jahannam. The tall man in the meadow was Ibrahim. The children who were around him are all those who were born and died in the natural state.'

"He said, 'One of the Muslims asked: 'Messenger of Allah, the children of the idolaters as well?'' The Messenger of Allah said, 'The children of the idolaters as well. As for the people who were half beautiful and half ugly, they are the people who mixed righteous actions with evil actions. Allah excused them.'"[37]

---

[37] Reported by Al-Bukhari, number: 6640.
Ibn Al-Qayyim (rahimahullah) said, in his book "Ar-Ruh" (print: Muhammad Ali Subaih, page: 86):
"This is a clear text regarding the punishment of Al-Barzakh, as the dreams of the prophets are revelation, which correspond to the actual affair."
And Al-Qurtubi said, in his book "At-Tadhkira", as it is in "Mukhtasr At-Tadhkirah" (print: Dar Al-Asimah, page 131): "Our scholars (rahmatullahi alaihim) said: 'There is no (hadith) clearer regarding the state of those that are punished in their graves than Al-Bukari's hadith, even if it was a dream, as the dreams of the prophets (alaihim assalaam) are revelation. The proof being Ibrahim's (alaihi assalaam) saying: 'O my son! I have seen in a dream that I am slaughtering you,' so his son

26. It is related that Abu Hurairah said:

كُنَّا نَمْشِي مَعَ رَسُولِ اللهِ صَلَّى اللهُ عَلَيْهِ وَسَلَّمَ ، فَمَرَرْنَا عَلَى قَبْرَيْنِ ، فَقَامَ ، فَقُمْنَا مَعَهُ ، فَجَعَلَ لَوْنُهُ يَتَغَيَّرُ حَتَّى رَعَدَ كُمُّ قَمِيصِهِ ، فَقُلْنَا : مَا لَكَ يَا نَبِيَّ اللهِ ؟ قَالَ : مَا تَسْمَعُونَ مَا أَسْمَعُ ؟ قُلْنَا : وَمَا ذَاكَ يَا نَبِيَّ اللهِ ؟ قَالَ : هَذَانِ رَجُلانِ يُعَذَّبَانِ فِي قُبُورِهِمَا عَذَابًا شَدِيدًا فِي ذَنْبٍ هَيِّنٍ ، قُلْنَا : مِمَّ ذَلِكَ يَا نَبِيَّ اللهِ ؟ قَالَ : كَانَ أَحَدُهُمَا لا يَسْتَنْزِهُ مِنَ الْبَوْلِ ، وَكَانَ الآخَرُ يُؤْذِي النَّاسَ بِلِسَانِهِ ، وَيَمْشِي بَيْنَهُمْ بِالنَّمِيمَةِ ، فَدَعَا بِجَرِيدَتَيْنِ مِنْ جَرَائِدِ النَّخْلِ ، فَجَعَلَ فِي كُلِّ قَبْرٍ وَاحِدَةً . قُلْنَا : وَهَلْ يَنْفَعُهُمَا ذَلِكَ يَا رَسُولَ اللهِ؟ قَالَ : نَعَمْ ، يُخَفِّفُ عَنْهُمَا مَا دَامَا رَطْبَتَيْنِ.

"We were walking with the Messenger of Allah (sallallahu alaihi wa sallam) when we passed two graves. Then he stood still and we stood with him. His color started to change and he rolled up his sleeves, so we said: 'What's the matter, oh Prophet of Allah?' He said: 'Don't you hear what I'm hearing?' We said: 'What is it, oh Prophet of Allah?' He said:

---

replies: 'O my father! Do that which you are commanded.''" (As-Saffat: 102).

'These two men are being severely punished in their graves for a relatively minor sin.' We said: 'For what are they punished, oh Prophet of Allah?' He said: 'One of them never used to clean urine from himself, and the other used to harm the people by his speech and walk amongst the people carrying tales.'

"So he called for two palm stalks and he put one into each grave. We said: 'Will this benefit them, oh Messenger of Allah?' He replied: 'Yes, it will lighten their punishment for as long as it remains moist.'"[38]

27. It is related from Ibn 'Abbas from the Prophet (sallallahu alaihi wa sallam):

مَرَّ النَّبِيُّ صَلَّى اللهُ عَلَيْهِ وَسَلَّمَ عَلَى قَبْرَيْنِ فَقَالَ إِنَّهُمَا لَيُعَذَّبَانِ، وَمَا يُعَذَّبَانِ مِنْ كَبِيرٍ - ثُمَّ قَالَ - بَلَى أَمَّا أَحَدُهُمَا فَكَانَ يَسْعَى بِالنَّمِيمَةِ، وَأَمَّا أَحَدُهُمَا فَكَانَ لاَ يَسْتَتِرُ مِنْ بَوْلِهِ . قَالَ ثُمَّ أَخَذَ عُودًا رَطْبًا فَكَسَرَهُ بِاثْنَتَيْنِ ثُمَّ غَرَزَ كُلَّ وَاحِدٍ مِنْهُمَا عَلَى قَبْرٍ، ثُمَّ قَالَ : ((لَعَلَّهُ يُخَفَّفُ عَنْهُمَا مَا لَمْ يَيْبَسَا)).

[38] Reported by Abu Hatim (3/106) in "Al-Ihsan". And Sheikh Muqbil declared it as "good" in "Al-Jami' As-Sahih mimma laisa fi As-Sahihain" (2/278-279).

"He passed by two graves whose inhabitants were being punished. He said, 'They are not being punished for anything very great. One of them used to go around slandering people and the other did not protect himself from urine.' Then he took a green palm branch, split it in two and then stuck one piece in each grave. Then he said: 'May it (their punishment) be lightened for them for as long as they (the palm branches) do not dry out.'"[39]

28. It is related that AbdurRahman bin Hasanah (radiallahu anhu) said:

انْطَلَقْتُ أَنَا وَعَمْرُو بْنُ الْعَاصِ، إِلَى النَّبِيِّ صَلَّى اللهُ عَلَيْهِ وَسَلَّمَ فَخَرَجَ وَمَعَهُ دَرَقَةٌ ثُمَّ اسْتَتَرَ بِهَا ثُمَّ بَالَ فَقُلْنَا انْظُرُوا إِلَيْهِ يَبُولُ كَمَا تَبُولُ الْمَرْأَةُ . فَسَمِعَ ذَلِكَ فَقَالَ : ((أَلَمْ تَعْلَمُوا مَا لَقِيَ صَاحِبُ بَنِي إِسْرَائِيلَ كَانُوا إِذَا أَصَابَهُمُ الْبَوْلُ قَطَعُوا مَا أَصَابَهُ الْبَوْلُ مِنْهُمْ فَنَهَاهُمْ فَعُذِّبَ فِي قَبْرِهِ)). قَالَ أَبُو دَاوُدَ قَالَ مَنْصُورٌ عَنْ أَبِي وَائِلٍ عَنْ أَبِي مُوسَى فِي هَذَا الْحَدِيثِ قَالَ : ((جِلْدَ أَحَدِهِمْ)) . وَقَالَ عَاصِمٌ عَنْ أَبِي وَائِلٍ عَنْ أَبِي مُوسَى عَنِ النَّبِيِّ صَلَّى اللهُ عَلَيْهِ وَسَلَّمَ قَالَ : ((جَسَدَ أَحَدِهِمْ)) .

[39] Reported by Al-Bukhari, number: 1312; and Muslim, number: 292.

"I and Amr bin Al-'Aas (radiallahu anhu) went to the Prophet (sallallahu alaihi wa sallam). He came out with a leather shield. He covered himself with it and urinated. Then we said: 'Look at him. He is urinating as a woman does.' The Prophet (sallallahu alaihi wa sallam) heard this and said: 'Do you not know what befell a person from amongst Banu Isra'il (the children of Israel)? When urine fell on them, they would cut off the place where the urine fell; but he (that person) forbade them (to do so), and so was punished in his grave.'"[40]

29. It is related from Abdullah bin Abbas that the Messenger of Allah (sallallahu alaihi wa sallam) said:

قَالَ رَسُولُ اللهِ - صَلَّى اللهُ عَلَيْهِ وَ سَلَّمَ : ((إِنَّ عَامَّةَ عَذَابِ الْقَبْرِ مِنَ الْبَوْلِ ، فَتَنَزَّهُوا مِنْهُ)) .

[40] Reported by Abu Dawud (1/42), An-Nisa'i (1/26), and Ibn Majah (1/124).
Sheikh Muqbil Al-Waadi'i (rahimahullah) said in "Al-Jami' As-Sahih mimma laisa fi As-Sahihain" [in the chapter of "The Punishment of the Deviant Mufti (1/43-44), the new print]: "This hadith is authentic in accordance with the requirements of the two scholars (i.e., Al-Bukhari and Muslim), even if there are some doubts concerning Abdul Wahid bin Ziyad's narration from Al-A'mash, as Muawiyyah and Wakee' followed him according to Imam Ahmad (4/196), and the hadith is from that which Ad-Daraqutni proscribed Al-Bukhari and Muslim to report."

"Verily, the majority of the punishments of the grave are due to urine, so remove it from yourselves."[41]

30. It is related from Abdullah bin Umar (radiallahu anhu) that he said:

قَالَ رَسُولُ اللهِ - صَلَّى اللهُ عَلَيْهِ وَ سَلَّمَ : ((إِنَّ الْمَيِّتَ يُعَذَّبُ فِي قَبْرِهِ، بِمَا نِيحَ عَلَيْهِ)) .

"The Messenger of Allah (sallallahu alaihi wa sallam) said: 'The deceased is punished due to the wailing done over him.'"[42]

31. It is related that Abu Hurairah said:

افْتَتَحْنَا خَيْبَرَ، وَلَمْ نَغْنَمْ ذَهَبًا وَلاَ فِضَّةً، إِنَّمَا غَنِمْنَا الْبَقَرَ وَالإِبِلَ وَالْمَتَاعَ وَالْحَوَائِطَ، ثُمَّ انْصَرَفْنَا مَعَ رَسُولِ اللهِ صَلَّى اللهُ عَلَيْهِ وَسَلَّمَ إِلَى وَادِي الْقُرَى، وَمَعَهُ عَبْدٌ لَهُ يُقَالُ لَهُ مِدْعَمٌ، أَهْدَاهُ لَهُ أَحَدُ بَنِي الضِّبَابِ، فَبَيْنَمَا هُوَ يَحُطُّ رَحْلَ

---

[41] Reported by Abd bin Hamid, Al-Bazzar, At-Tabarani in "Al-Kabir", Ad-Daraqutni, and Abu Na'im.
Sheikh Al-Albani (rahimahullah) declared it authentic in "Sahih Al-Jami'", number 2098.

[42] Reported by Al-Bukhari, number: 1230; and Muslim, number: 927.
As it was in "Kitabul Jina'iz" by Al-Albani, page: 40.

رَسُولِ اللهِ صَلَّى اللهُ عَلَيْهِ وَسَلَّمَ إِذْ جَاءَهُ سَهْمٌ عَائِرٌ حَتَّى أَصَابَ ذَلِكَ الْعَبْدَ، فَقَالَ النَّاسُ هَنِيئًا لَهُ الشَّهَادَةُ. فَقَالَ رَسُولُ اللهِ صَلَّى اللهُ عَلَيْهِ وَسَلَّمَ : ((كَلَّا ، وَالَّذِي نَفْسِي بِيَدِهِ، إِنَّ الشَّمْلَةَ الَّتِي أَصَابَهَا يَوْمَ خَيْبَرَ مِنَ الْمَغَانِمِ لَمْ تُصِبْهَا الْمَقَاسِمُ لَتَشْتَعِلُ عَلَيْهِ نَارًا)). فَجَاءَ رَجُلٌ حِينَ سَمِعَ ذَلِكَ مِنَ النَّبِيِّ صلى الله عليه وسلم بِشِرَاكٍ أَوْ بِشِرَاكَيْنِ، فَقَالَ هَذَا شَيْءٌ كُنْتُ أَصَبْتُهُ. فَقَالَ رَسُولُ اللهِ صَلَّى اللهُ عَلَيْهِ وسلم : ((شِرَاكٌ أَوْ شِرَاكَانِ مِنْ نَارٍ)).

"When we conquered Khaibar, we gained neither gold nor silver as booty, but we gained cows, camels, goods and gardens. Then we departed with Allah's Messenger (sallallahu alaihi wa sallam) to the valley of Al-Qura, and at that time, Allah's Messenger (sallallahu alaihi wa sallam) had a slave called Mid`am who had been presented to him by one of Banu Ad-Dibbab. While the slave was dismounting the saddle of Allah's Messenger (sallallahu alaihi wa sallam), an arrow, the thrower of which was unknown, came and hit him. The people said, 'Congratulations to him for the martyrdom.' Allah's Messenger said, 'No, by Him in Whose Hand is my soul, the sheet of cloth which he had taken (illegally) on the day of Khaibar from the booty before the distribution of the booty, has

become a flame of fire burning him.' On hearing that from the Prophet (sallallahu alaihi wa sallam), a man brought one or two leather straps of shoes and said, 'These are things I took.' On that, Allah's Messenger (sallallahu alaihi wa sallam) said, 'This is a strap, or these are two straps of fire.'"[43]

32. It is related that Jabir bin Abdullah Al-Ansari (radiallahu anhu) said:

مَاتَ رَجُلٌ فَغَسَّلْنَاهُ ، وَ كَفَّنَّاهُ ، وَ حَنَّطْنَاهُ ، وَ وَضَعْنَاهُ لِرَسُولِ اللهِ – صَلَّى اللهُ عَلَيْهِ وَ سَلَّمَ – حَيْثُ تُوْضَعُ الْجَنَائِزَ ، عِنْدَ مَقَامِ جِبْرِيْلَ ، ثُمَّ آذَنَّا رَسُولَ اللهِ – صَلَّى اللهُ عَلَيْهِ وَ سَلَّمَ – لِلصَّلَاةِ عَلَيْهِ ، فَجَاءَ مَعَنَا ، فَتَخَطَّى خُطَىً ، ثُمَّ قَالَ : ((لَعَلَّ عَلَى صَاحِبِكُمْ دَيْنًا ؟)) . قَالُوا : نَعَمْ ، دِيْنَارَانِ . فَتَخَلَّفَ ، قَالَ : ((صَلُّوا عَلَى صَاحِبِكُمْ)) . فَقَالَ لَهُ رَجُلٌ مِنَّا ، يُقَالُ لَهُ : أَبُو قَتَادَةَ : يَا رَسُولَ اللهِ هُمَا عَلَيَّ . فَجَعَلَ رَسُولَ اللهِ – صَلَّى اللهُ عَلَيْهِ وَ سَلَّمَ – يَقُولُ :

[43] Reported by Al-Bukhari, number: 3993; and Muslim, number: 115.

((هُـمَـا عَـلَـيْـكَ ، وَ فِـي مَـالِـكَ ، وَالْـمَـيِّـتُ مِـنْـهُـمَـا بَـرِيءٌ ؟)) . فَـقَـالَ : نَـعَـمْ . فَـصَـلَّـى عَـلَـيْـهِ .

فَـجَـعَـلَ رَسُـولُ اللهِ - صَـلَّـى اللهُ عَـلَـيْـهِ وَ سَـلَّـمَ - إِذَا لَـقِـيَ أَبَـا قَـتَـادَةَ ، يَـقُـولُ : وَ فِـي رِوَايَـةٍ : ثُـمَّ لَـقِـيَـهُ مِـنَ الْـغَـدِ ، فَـقَـالَ : ((مَـا صَـنَـعَـتِ الـدِّيْـنَـارَانِ ؟)) . قَـالَ : يَـا رَسُـولَ اللهِ ، إِنَّـمَـا مَـاتَ أَمْـسِ . حَـتَّـى كَـانَ آخِـرَ ذَلِـكَ ، وَ فِـي الـرِّوَايَـةِ الأُخْـرَى : ثُـمَّ لَـقِـيَـهُ مِـنَ الْـغَـدِ ، فَـقَـالَ : مَـا فَـعَـلَ الـدِّيْـنَـارَانِ ؟ قَـالَ : قَـدْ قَـضَـيْـتُـهُـمَـا يَـا رَسُـولَ اللهِ . قَـالَ : ((الْآنَ حِـيـنَ بَـرَدَتْ عَـلَـيْـهِ جِـلْـدُهُ)) .

"A man died, so we washed him, we enshrouded him, we embalmed him, and we placed him at the place for the funeral prayer for the Messenger of Allah, at the Standing Place of Jibril, then we called the Messenger of Allah to pray for him. He came with us and then he skipped a step, then he said: 'Perhaps your companion has a debt?' They said: 'Yes, two dinars.' So he began to fall behind and he said: 'Pray for your companion.' A man from amongst us, called Abu Qatada, said to him: 'O Messenger of Allah, they are on me!' So the Messenger of Allah said: 'They are on you and your wealth, and the deceased is free from them?' and he

said: 'Yes.' So he (the Messenger of Allah) prayed over him.

"The Messenger of Allah began to say, whenever he saw Abu Qatada (and in another narration: when he saw him the next day): 'What have you done about the two dinars?' He said: 'O Messenger of Allah, he just died yesterday.' He continued like that, until he finally said: 'I paid it, O Messenger of Allah.' He (the Prophet) said: 'Now his flesh will begin to cool.'"[44]

33. It is related from Samurah bin Jundub (radiallahu anhu) that the Prophet (sallallahu alaihi wa sallam) prayed a funeral prayer (and in another narration: prayed the morning prayer).

فَلَمَّا انْصَرَفَ قَالَ : ((أَهَاهُنَا مِنْ آلِ فُلَانٍ أَحَدٌ ؟)) ، فَسَكَتَ الْقَوْمُ ، وَ كَانَ إِذَا ابْتَدَأَهُمْ بِشَيْءٍ ، سَكَتُوا ، فَقَالَ ذَلِكَ مِرَارًا ، ثَلَاثًا ، لَا يُجِيبُ أَحَدٌ ، فَقَالَ رَجُلٌ : هُوَ ذَا . قَالَ : فَقَامَ رَجُلٌ ، يَجُرُّ إِزَارَهُ مِنْ مُؤَخَّرِ

---

[44] Reported by Al-Hakim (2/58), and the wording of the hadith is his; Al-Bayhaqi (6/74-75); At-Tiyalasi, number: 1673; and Ahmad (3/330), with a "good" chain of narration, as stated by Al-Haithami (3/39).
Al-Hakim said: "authentic chain of narration," and Adh-Dhahabi agreed with him.
And it is similarly reported in "Ahkam Al-Jana'iz" by Sheikh Al-Albani, page: 27.

النَّاسِ ، فَقَالَ لَهُ النَّبِيُّ - صَلَّى اللهُ عَلَيْهِ وَ سَلَّمَ - : ((مَا مَنَعَكَ فِي الْمَرَّتَيْنِ الْأُولَيَيْنِ أَنْ تَكُونَ أَجَبْتَنِي ؟ أَ مَا إِنِّي لَمْ أُنَوِّهُ بِاسْمِكَ إِلَّا لِخَيْرٍ ، إِنَّ فُلَانًا - لِرَجُلٍ مِنْهُمْ - مَأْسُورٌ بِدَيْنِهِ عَنِ الْجَنَّةِ ، فَإِنْ شِئْتُمْ فَافْدُوهُ ، وَ إِنْ شِئْتُمْ فَأَسْلِمُوهُ إِلَى عَذَابِ اللهِ)) . فَلَوْ رَأَيْتَ أَهْلَهُ ، وَ مَنْ يَتَحَرَّوْنَ أَمْرَهُ ، قَامُوا ، فَقَضَوْا عَنْهُ ، حَتَّى مَا أَحَدٌ يَطْلُبُهُ بِشَيْءٍ .

When he left, he said: "Is there anyone here from the family of so and so?" The people were silent, and when he began (to say) something, they were quiet. So he repeated it three times, but no one answered, so a man said: "He is." Then a man, at the back of the people, stood, dragging his lower garment, then the Prophet (sallallahu alaihi wa sallam) said to him: "What stopped you from answering me the first two times? I only called your name to tell you something good. So and so has been detained from entering paradise due to a debt, so if you wish then pay off the debt, and if you wish then leave him to Allah's punishment. So if you see any of his family or those who have concern for his

situation then let them pay (the debt) until there is no one left asking him for anything."[45]

34. It is related that Salama bin Al-Akwa said:

قَالَ كُنَّا جُلُوسًا عِنْدَ النَّبِيِّ صَلَّى اللهُ عَلَيْهِ وَسَلَّمَ إِذْ أُتِيَ بِجَنَازَةٍ، فَقَالُوا صَلِّ عَلَيْهَا. فَقَالَ : ((هَلْ عَلَيْهِ دَيْنٌ)). قَالُوا لاَ. قَالَ : ((فَهَلْ تَرَكَ شَيْئًا)). قَالُوا لاَ. فَصَلَّى عَلَيْهِ ثُمَّ أُتِيَ بِجَنَازَةٍ أُخْرَى، فَقَالُوا يَا رَسُولَ اللهِ . صَلِّ عَلَيْهَا. قَالَ : ((هَلْ عَلَيْهِ دَيْنٌ)). قِيلَ نَعَمْ. قَالَ : ((فَهَلْ تَرَكَ شَيْئًا)). قَالُوا ثَلاَثَةَ دَنَانِيرَ. فَصَلَّى عَلَيْهَا، ثُمَّ أُتِيَ بِالثَّالِثَةِ، فَقَالُوا صَلِّ عَلَيْهَا. قَالَ : ((هَلْ تَرَكَ شَيْئًا)). قَالُوا لاَ. قَالَ : ((فَهَلْ عَلَيْهِ دَيْنٌ)). قَالُوا ثَلاَثَةُ دَنَانِيرَ. قَالَ : ((صَلُّوا عَلَى صَاحِبِكُمْ)). قَالَ أَبُو قَتَادَةَ صَلِّ عَلَيْهِ يَا رَسُولَ اللهِ ، وَعَلَيَّ دَيْنُهُ. فَصَلَّى عَلَيْهِ.

"Once, while we were sitting in the company of Prophet (sallallahu alaihi wa sallam), a dead man

---

[45] Reported by Abu Dawud, An-Nisa'I (2/233), Al-Hakim (2/25 and 26), Al-Bayhaqi (6/4)(76), At-Tiyalasi, number: 891 and 892; and Ahmad (5/11, 13, and 20).
Sheikh Al-Albani (rahimahullah) declared it authentic in "Ahkam Al-Jana'iz", page: 26.

was brought. They said: 'May you lead the funeral prayer for the deceased?' He said, 'Is he in debt?' The people replied, 'No.' He said, 'Has he left any wealth?' They said, 'No.' So, he led his funeral prayer.

"Another dead man was brought and the people said, 'O Messenger of Allah (sallallahu alaihi wa sallam) lead his funeral prayer.' The Prophet said, 'Is he in debt?' They said, 'Yes.' He said, 'Has he left any wealth?' They said, 'Three Dinars.' So, he led the prayer.

"Then a third dead man was brought and the people said (to the Prophet), 'Please lead his funeral prayer.' He said, 'Has he left any wealth?' They said, 'No.' He asked, 'Is he in debt?' They said, 'Yes! Three Diners.' He (refused to pray and) said, 'Then pray for your (dead) companion.' Then a man from the Ansar called Abu Qatada said, 'O Messenger of Allah! Lead his funeral prayer, and I will pay his debt.' So, he led the prayer."[46]

35. It is related that Abu Hurairah (radiallahu anhu) said that The Messenger of Allah (sallallahu alaihi wa sallam) said:

[46] Reported by Al-Bukhari, number: 2169; and Ahmad and Nisaa'i. As it is reported in "Ahkam Al-Jana'iz" by Sheikh Al-Albani, page: 111.

قَالَ رَسُولُ اللهِ - صَلَّى اللهُ عَلَيْهِ وَ سَلَّمَ - : ((نَفْسُ الْمُؤْمِنِ مُعَلَّقَةٌ بِدَيْنِهِ ، حَتَّى يُقْضَى عَنْهُ)).

"The believer's soul is attached to his debt until it is paid off for him."[47]

36. It is related from Sa'd bin Atwal that his brother died, leaving behind three hundred Dirham and dependents. He said:

إِنَّ أَخَاكَ مَحْبُوسٌ بِدَيْنِهِ ، فَاذْهَبْ ، فَاقْضِ عَنْهُ. فَذَهَبْتُ ، فَقَضَيْتُ عَنْهُ ، ثُمَّ جِئْتُ ، قُلْتُ : يَا رَسُولَ اللهِ قَدْ قَضَيْتُ عَنْهُ ، إِلَّا دِينَارَيْنِ ادَّعَتْهُمَا امْرَأَةٌ ، وَلَيْسَتْ لَهَا بَيِّنَةٌ ، قَالَ : ((أَعْطِهَا ؛ فَإِنَّهَا مُحِقَّةٌ – وَ فِي رِوَايَةٍ : صَادِقَةٌ)).

"I wanted to spend (his money) on his dependents, but the Prophet (sallallahu alaihi wa sallam) said: 'Your brother is being detained by his debt, so pay it off for him.'" He said: "O Messenger of Allah (sallallahu alaihi wa sallam), I have paid it off apart from two Dinar, which a woman is claiming but she has no proof." He said: "Give them to her for she is

[47] Reported by Ahmad, At-Tirmidhi, Ibn Majah and Al-Hakim. Sheikh Al-Albani declared it authentic in his book "Sahih Al-Jami'", number: 6779.

telling the truth (or in another narration: *she is honest*)."[48]

37. It is related that Anas bin Malik (radiallahu anhu) related that the Prophet (sallallahu alaihi wa sallam) said:

لَيْلَةَ أُسْرِيَ بِي رَأَيْتُ قَوْمًا تُقْرَضُ أَلْسِنَتُهُمْ بِمَقَارِيضَ مِنْ نَارٍ - أَوْ قَالَ: مِنْ حَدِيدٍ - قُلْتُ: مَنْ هَؤُلَاءِ يَا جِبْرِيلُ ؟! قَالَ: خُطَبَاءُ أُمَّتِكَ)) . وَ فِي لَفْظٍ: ((أَتَيْتُ عَلَى سَمَاءِ الدُّنْيَا، لَيْلَةَ أُسْرِيَ بِي، فَرَأَيْتُ فِيهَا رِجَالًا تُقَطَّعُ أَلْسِنَتُهُمْ، وَ شِفَاهُهُمْ بِمَقَارِيضَ مِنْ نَارٍ، فَقُلْتُ: يَا جِبْرِيلُ! مَا هَؤُلَاءِ ؟ قَالَ: هَؤُلَاءِ خُطَبَاءُ مِن أُمَّتِكَ)) .

"The night that I was ascended, I saw a people who were tearing their tongues with scissors of fire (or he said: *of steel*), so I said: 'Who are they, O Jibril!?' He said: 'They are the preachers of your Ummah.'"

[48] Reported by Ibn Majah (2/82), Ahmad (4/136 and 5/7), and Al-Bayhaqi (10/142).
Sheikh Al-Albani said (rahimahullah): "One of its two narrations is authentic."
See "Kitab Al-Jana'iz", page: 26.

"And in another wording: 'I came to the sky of the Dunya the night that I was ascended, and I saw men cutting their tongues and their lips with scissors of fire, so I said: 'O Jibril, who are they?' He said: 'They are preachers from your Ummah.'"[49]

[49] Reported by Abu Ya'la (7/118 and 180). Sheikh Muqbil Al-Wadi'i (rahimahullah) declared it to be authentic in "As-Sahih Al-Musnad mimma laisa fis Sahihain". Sheikh Al-Albani (rahimahullah) also declared it to be authentic.

CHAPTER 5: REASONS FOR BEING SAVED FROM THE PUNISHMENT OF THE GRAVE

38. It is related that Abdullah bin Mas'ood said that the Messenger of Allah said:

سُـورَةُ تَـبَـارَكَ ، هِـيَ الْـمَـانِـعَـةُ مِـنْ عَـذَابِ الْـقَـبْـرِ

"Surah Tabarak is a protection from the punishment of the grave." [50]

39. It is related from Abu Hurayrah (radiallahu anhu) that the Messenger of Allah (sallallahu alaihi wa sallam) said:

إِنَّ الْمَيِّتَ إِذَا وُضِعَ فِي قَبْرِهِ ، إِنَّهُ يَسْمَعُ خَفْقَ نِعَالِهِمْ حِينَ يُوَلُّونَ عَنْهُ ، فَإِنْ كَانَ مُؤْمِنًا كَانَتِ الصَّلاةُ عِنْدَ رَأْسِهِ ، وَكَانَ الصِّيَامُ عَنْ يَمِينِهِ ، وَكَانَتِ الزَّكَاةُ عَنْ شِمَـالِـهِ ، وَكَانَ فِعْلُ الْخَيْرَاتِ مِنَ الصَّدَقَةِ وَالصِّلَةِ وَالْمَعْرُوفِ وَالإِحْسَانِ إِلَى النَّاسِ عِنْدَ رِجْلَيْهِ ، فَيُؤْتَى مِنْ قِبَلِ رَأْسِهِ ، فَتَقُولُ الصَّلاةُ : مَا قِبَلِي مَدْخَلٌ ، ثُـمَّ يُـؤْتَـى عَـنْ

[50] Reported by Abu Sheikh in "Tabaqat Al-Asbahaniyin", number: 264, and Al-Hakim (2/498).
Sheikh Al-Albani (rahimahullah) declared it to be good in "As-Silsilah As-Sahihah", number: 1140.

يَـمِـينِـهِ ، فَـيَـقُـولُ الـصِّـيَـامُ : مَـا قِـبَـلِـي مَـدْخَـلٌ. ثُمَّ يُؤْتَى مِنْ يَسَارِهِ ، فَتَقُولُ الزَّكَاةُ : مَا قِبَلِي مَدْخَلٍ ، ثُمَّ يُؤْتَى مِنْ قِبَلِ رِجْلَيْهِ ، فَتَقُولُ فِعْلُ الْخَيْرَاتِ مِنَ الصَّدَقَةِ وَالْمَعْرُوفِ وَالإِحْسَانِ إِلَى النَّاسِ : مَا قِبَلِي مَدْخَلٌ ، فَيُقَالُ لَهُ : اجْلِسْ ، فَيَجْلِسُ، وَ قَـدْ مُـثِّـلَـتْ لَـهُ الـشَّـمْـسُ ، وَ قَـدْ أُدْنِـيَـتْ لِـلْـغُـرُوبِ ، فَـيُـقَـالُ لَـهُ: أَرَأَيْتُكَ هَذَا الرَّجُلَ الَّذِي كَانَ فِيكُمْ مَا تَقُولُ فِيهِ ؟ وَ مَـاذَا تَـشْـهَـدُ بِـهِ عَـلَـيْـهِ ؟ فَيَقُولُ : دَعُونِي حَتَّى أُصَلِّيَ ، فَـيَـقُـولُـونَ : : إِنَّكَ سَتَفْعَلُ ، أَخْبِرْنَا عَمَّا نَسْأَلُكَ عَنْهُ ، أَ رَأَيْـتَـكَ هَـذَا الـرَّجُـلَ الَّـذِي كَـانَ فِـيـكُـمْ، مَـا تَـقُـولُ فِـيـهِ ؟ وَ مَـاذَا تَـشْـهَـدُ عَـلَـيْـهِ ؟ قَـالَ : فَـيَـقُـولُ : مُـحَـمَّـدٌ ، أَشْـهَـدُ أَنَّـهُ رَسُـولُ اللهِ ، وَ أَنَّـهُ جَـاءَ بِـالْـحَـقِّ مِـنْ عِـنْـدِ اللهِ . فَـيُـقَـالُ لَـهُ : عَـلَـى ذَلِـكَ حَـيِـيْـتَ ، وَ عَـلَـى ذَلِـكَ مِـتَّ ، وَ عَـلَـى ذَلِـكَ تُـبْـعَـثُ إِنْ شَـاءَ اللهُ . ثُـمَّ يُـفْـتَـحُ لَـهُ بَـابٌ مِـنْ أَبْـوَابِ الْـجَـنَّـةِ ، فَـيُـقَـالُ لَـهُ : هَـذَا مَـقْـعَـدُكَ مِـنْـهَـا ، وَ مَـا أَعَـدَّ اللهُ لَـكَ فِـيـهَـا . فَـيَـزْدَادُ غِـبْـطَـةً وَ سُـرُورًا ، .... ، ثُـمَّ يُـفْـسَـحُ لَـهُ فِـي قَـبْـرِهِ سَـبْـعُـونَ ذِرَاعًـا ، وَ يُـنَـوَّرُ لَـهُ فِـيـهِ)) .

"When the deceased is placed in his grave, he hears the footsteps of the people as they leave. If he was a believer, the prayer will be at his head, the fast will be on his right, the zakah will be on his left, and his good deeds of charity, prayer, good, and benevolence to others will be at his legs. He will be approached from the direction of his head, and the prayer will say: 'There's no entry here.' and he will be approached from his right and the fast will say: 'There's no entry here.' and he will be approached from the left and the zakah will say: 'There's no entry here.' and he will be approached from the direction of his legs and good deeds of charity, prayer, good, and benevolence to others will say: 'There's no entry here.'

"Then it will be said to him: 'Sit' so he will sit. Then the likeness of the sun will be made to appear as it is setting, and it will be said to him: 'Did you see this man that used to be amongst you, what do you say about him? And what do you testify concerning him?' He will say: 'Leave me so that I may pray.' They will say: 'You will, (first) tell me about what we ask you of concerning this man. Did you see this man that used to be amongst you, what do you say about him? And what do you testify concerning him?' So he said: 'Muhammad, I testify that he is the messenger of Allah and that he brought the truth from Allah.' Then it will be said to him: 'You lived by this, died by this and by it you shall be resurrected, inshallah.' Then a door from the doors

of Jannah is opened and it is said to him: 'This is your place that Allah has prepared for you in it.' So he becomes exultant and joyous,...then his grave is expanded seventy by seventy cubits and his grave will be lit up for him..."[51]

40. It is related that Al-Miqdam bin Ma'di Karib related that the Messenger of Allah (sallallahu alaihi wa sallam) said:

لِلشَّهِيدِ عِنْدَ اللهِ خِصَالٌ :

- يَغْفِرُ لَهُ فِي أَوَّلِ دُفْعَةٍ مِنْ دَمِهِ .
- وَ يُرَى مَقْعَدَهُ مِنَ الْجَنَّةِ .
- وَ يُحَلَّى حِلْيَةَ الْإِيمَانِ .
- وَ يُزَوَّجُ اثْنَتَيْنِ وَ سَبْعِينَ زَوْجَةً مِنَ الْحُورِ الْعِينِ .
- وَ يُجَارُ مِنْ عَذَابِ الْقَبْرِ .
- وَ يَأْمَنُ مِنَ الْفَزَعِ الْأَكْبَرِ .

---

[51] Reported by Ibn Hibbam (7/380)(3113), checking by Shu'aib, and checking by Al-Albani (5/95)(3103); Abdurrazzaq, number: 6703; Ibn Abi Shaibah; Hannad bin As-Sirri in "Az-Zuhd", number: 338; At-Tabarani in "At-Tafsir"; Al-Hakim (1/379-380); and Al-Bayhaqi in "Al-I'tiqaad", page: 220, in "Affirmation of the Punishment of the Grave", number: 67.
Sheikh Al-Albani declared it to be "good" in "Sahih At-Targhib wat Tarhib", number: 3561, and Shu'aib Al-Arna'ut.

- وَ يُوضَعُ عَلَى رَأْسِهِ تَاجُ الْوَقَارِ، الْيَاقُوتَةُ مِنْهُ خَيْرٌ مِنَ الدُّنْيَا وَ مَا فِيهَا.
- وَ يُشَفَّعُ فِي سَبْعِينَ إِنْسَانًا مِنْ أَهْلِ بَيْتِهِ.

"The martyr has certain characteristics:

- **He is forgiven from the first drop of his blood.**
- **He is shown his place in Jannah.**
- **He wears the jewelry of *īmān*.**
- **He is married to seventy two wives from the Hurul Ein.**
- **He is protected from the punishment of the grave.**
- **He is saved from the Great Panic.**
- **A crown of dignity is placed on his head; the ruby on it is better than the World and all that is in it.**
- **He seeks intercession for seventy of his family."[52]**

---

52 Reported by Ahmad and At-Tirmidhi, number: 1663; Ibn Majah, number: 2799; Al-Bayhaqi in "Ash-Sha'b, and Ibn Asakir in "At-Tarikh". Sheikh Al-Albani (rahimahullah) declared it to be authentic in "As-Silsilah As-Sahihah", number: 3213.

41. It is related that Uqbah bin Amir Al-Juhani said that the Messenger of Allah (sallallahu alaihi wa sallam) said:

إِنَّ الصَّدَقَةَ لَتُطْفِئُ عَنْ أَهْلِهَا حَرَّ الْقُبُورِ ، وَ إِنَّمَا يَسْتَظِلُّ الْمُؤْمِنُ يَوْمَ الْقِيَامَةِ ، فِي صَدَقَتِهِ .

"Charity quenches the heat of the grave for its inhabitant. And the believer will only find shade on the Day of Judgment under the shade of his charity."[53]

42. It is related that Anas bin Malik said that the Messenger of Allah (sallallahu alaihi wa sallam) said:

سَبْعٌ يَجْرِي لِلْعَبْدِ أَجْرُهُنَّ ، وَ هُوَ فِي قَبْرِهِ بَعْدَ مَوْتِهِ :

- مَنْ عَلَّمَ عِلْمًا .
- أَوْ أَجْرَى نَهْرًا .
- أَوْ حَفَرَ بِئْرًا .
- أَوْ غَرَسَ نَخْلًا .

[53] Reported by At-Tabarani in "Al-Kabir" (17/286) (787-788), and Al-Bayhaqi in "Ash-Sha'b".
Sheikh Al-Albani declared its chain of narration in "As-Silsilah As-Sahihah", number: 3484.

- أَوْ بَنَى مَسْجِدًا .
- أَوْ وَرَّثَ مُصْحَفًا .
- أَوْ تَرَكَ وَلَدًا ، يَسْتَغْفِرُ لَهُ بَعْدَ مَوْتِهِ .

"Seven continue on for the slave whilst he is in his grave:

Someone who taught something;

Or sprung a river;

Or dug a well;

Or planted a date tree;

Or built a masjid;

Or left behind a copy of the Quran;

Or left behind a son who seeks forgiveness for him after his death."[54]

---

[54] Reported by Al-Bazar and Samawaihi.
Sheikh Al-Albani declared it good in "Sahih Al-Jami'", number: 3602.

CHAPTER 6: SEEKING REFUGE IN ALLAH FROM THE PUNISHMENT OF THE GRAVE

43. It is related that Abu Hurairah (radiallahu anhu) said:

كَـانَ رَسُـولُ اللهِ - صَـلَّـى اللهُ عَـلَـيْـهِ وَ سَـلَّـمَ - يَـسْـتَـعِـيـذُ مِـنْ عَـذَابِ الْـقَـبْـرِ .

"The Messenger of Allah (sallallahu alaihi wa sallam) used to seek refuge in Allah from the punishment of the grave."[55]

44. It is related that Zaid bin Thabit Al-Ansari said that,

بَيْنَمَا النَّبِيُّ صَلَّى اللهُ عَلَيْهِ وَسَلَّمَ فِي حَائِطٍ لِبَنِي النَّجَّارِ عَلَى بَغْلَةٍ لَهُ وَنَحْنُ مَعَهُ إِذْ حَادَتْ بِهِ فَكَادَتْ تُلْقِيهِ وَإِذَا أَقْبُرٌ سِتَّةٌ أَوْ خَمْسَةٌ أَوْ أَرْبَعَةٌ – قَالَ كَذَا كَانَ يَقُولُ الْجُرَيْرِيُّ – فَقَالَ : ((مَنْ يَعْرِفُ أَصْحَابَ هَذِهِ الأَقْبُرِ)) . فَقَالَ رَجُلٌ أَنَا . قَالَ : ((فَمَتَى مَاتَ هَؤُلاَءِ)) . قَالَ مَاتُوا فِي الإِشْرَاكِ . فَقَالَ : ((إِنَّ هَذِهِ الأُمَّةَ تُبْتَلَى فِي قُبُورِهَا فَلَوْلاَ أَنْ لاَ تَدَافَنُوا

[55] Reported by Muslim, number: 585.

لَدَعَوْتُ اللهَ أَنْ يُسْمِعَكُمْ مِنْ عَذَابِ الْقَبْرِ الَّذِي أَسْمَعُ مِنْهُ)) . ثُمَّ أَقْبَلَ عَلَيْنَا بِوَجْهِهِ فَقَالَ : ((تَعَوَّذُوا بِاللهِ مِنْ عَذَابِ النَّارِ)) . قَالُوا نَعُوذُ بِاللهِ مِنْ عَذَابِ النَّارِ فَقَالَ : ((تَعَوَّذُوا بِاللهِ مِنْ عَذَابِ الْقَبْرِ)) . قَالُوا نَعُوذُ بِاللهِ مِنْ عَذَابِ الْقَبْرِ . قَالَ : ((تَعَوَّذُوا بِاللهِ مِنَ الْفِتَنِ مَا ظَهَرَ مِنْهَا وَمَا بَطَنَ)) . قَالُوا نَعُوذُ بِاللهِ مِنَ الْفِتَنِ مَا ظَهَرَ مِنْهَا وَمَا بَطَنَ قَالَ : ((تَعَوَّذُوا بِاللهِ مِنْ فِتْنَةِ الدَّجَّالِ)) . قَالُوا نَعُوذُ بِاللهِ مِنْ فِتْنَةِ الدَّجَّالِ .

One day the Prophet (sallallahu alaihi wa sallam) was in the gardens of Bani An-Najjar, riding upon his pony, and we were with him. It strayed and he almost fell. He found six, five, or four graves there. He said: "Who amongst you knows about those lying in the graves?" A person said: "I do." He (the Prophet) said: "When did they die?" He said: "They died during the polytheist time." He said: "Indeed this nation will be tested in their graves. If it were not for the fact that you would stop burying (your dead in the graves), I would have asked Allah to make you hear what I can hear from the punishment of the grave!" Then turning his face towards us, he said: "Seek refuge with Allah from the punishment of Hell." They said: "We seek refuge with Allah from the punishment of Hell." He said: "Seek

refuge with Allah from the punishment of the grave." They said: "We seek refuge with Allah from the punishment of the grave." He said: "Seek refuge with Allah from the trials, that which is apparent from them and that which is invisible." They said: "We seek refuge with Allah from the trials, that which is apparent from them and that which is invisible." And he said: "Seek refuge with Allah from the trial of the *Dajjal*." And they said: "We seek refuge with Allah from the trial of the *Dajjal*."[56]

45. It is related that Amr bin Shu'aib related from his father that his grandfather said: "I heard the Prophet (sallallahu alaihi wa sallam) say:

اللَّهُمَّ إِنِّي أَعُوذُ بِكَ مِنَ الْكَسَلِ ، وَ الْهَرَمِ ، وَ الْمَغْرَمِ، وَالْمَأْثَمِ ، وَ أَعُوذُ بِكَ مِنْ فِتْنَةِ الْمَسِيحِ الدَّجَّالِ، وَ أَعُوذُ بِكَ مِنْ عَذَابِ الْقَبْرِ، وَ أَعُوذُ بِكَ مِنْ عَذَابِ النَّارِ .

'O Allah, I seek refuge in you from laziness, decrepitude, debt, and sin, and I seek refuge in You from the trial of the *Masih Ad-Dajjal*, and I seek refuge in you from the punishment of the grave, and

[56] Reported by Muslim, number: 2867.

I seek refuge in you from the punishment of the fire.'"[57]

46. It is related that Abdullah bin Mas'ood reported that Umm Habiba, the wife of the Prophet (sallallahu alaihi wa sallam), said:

اللَّهُمَّ مَتِّعْنِي بِزَوْجِي رَسُولِ اللهِ صَلَّى اللهُ عَلَيْهِ وَسَلَّمَ وَبِأَبِي أَبِي سُفْيَانَ وَبِأَخِي مُعَاوِيَةَ . قَالَ فَقَالَ النَّبِيُّ صَلَّى اللهُ عَلَيْهِ وَسَلَّمَ : ((وَلَوْ كُنْتِ سَأَلْتِ اللهَ أَنْ يُعِيذَكِ مِنْ عَذَابٍ فِي النَّارِ أَوْ عَذَابٍ فِي الْقَبْرِ كَانَ خَيْرًا وَأَفْضَلَ)) .

"O Allah, enable me to derive benefit from my husband, the Messenger of Allah (sallallahu alaihi wa sallam), and from my father Abu Sufyan and from my brother Mu'awiya." The Prophet (sallallahu alaihi wa sallam) said: "...If you were to ask Allah to provide you refuge from the torment of the Hellfire, or from the torment of the grave, it would be better."[58]

---

[57] Reported by Ahmad (11/346-347)(6734). An-Nisaa'i in "Al-Mujtaba" (8/269)(5490) and in "Al-Kubra" (7392).

[58] Reported by Muslim, number: 2663.

47. It is related from Ibn Abbas (radiallahu anhu) that the Messenger of Allah used to teach them this supplication as he would a chapter from the Quran, saying:

قُولُوا

- اللَّهُمَّ إِنَّا نَعُوذُ بِكَ مِنْ عَذَابِ جَهَنَّمَ
- وَأَعُوذُ بِكَ مِنْ عَذَابِ الْقَبْرِ
- وَأَعُوذُ بِكَ مِنْ فِتْنَةِ الْمَسِيحِ الدَّجَّالِ
- وَأَعُوذُ بِكَ مِنْ فِتْنَةِ الْمَحْيَا وَالْمَمَاتِ .

"Say:

- **'O Allah, we seek refuge in you from the punishment of *Jahannam* (the hellfire).'**
- **'And I seek refuge in you from the punishment of the grave.'**
- **'And I seek refuge in you from the trials of the *Masih Ad-Dajjal*.'**
- **'And I seek refuge from the trials of life and death.'"**[59]

[59] Reported by Muslim, number: 590.

48. It is related that Abu Huraira said: The Messenger of Allah (sallallahu alaihi wa sallam) said:

إِذَا فَرَغَ أَحَدُكُمْ مِنَ التَّشَهُّدِ الآخِرِ فَلْيَتَعَوَّذْ بِاللهِ مِنْ أَرْبَعٍ:

- مِنْ عَذَابِ جَهَنَّمَ
- وَمِنْ عَذَابِ الْقَبْرِ
- وَمِنْ فِتْنَةِ الْمَحْيَا وَالْمَمَاتِ
- وَمِنْ شَرِّ الْمَسِيحِ الدَّجَّالِ

"When any one of you completes the last *tashahhud*, he should seek refuge with Allah from four (trials):

- **from the punishment of Hell,**
- **from the punishment of the grave,**
- **from the trials of life and death,**
- **and from the evil trials of *Masih Ad-Dajjal*."[60]**

49. It is related that Muslim bin Abi Bakra said:

---

[60] Reported by Muslim, number: 590.

كَانَ أَبِي يَقُولُ فِي دُبُرِ الصَّلاَةِ اللَّهُمَّ إِنِّي أَعُوذُ بِكَ مِنَ الْكُفْرِ وَالْفَقْرِ وَعَذَابِ الْقَبْرِ فَكُنْتُ أَقُولُهُنَّ فَقَالَ أَبِي أَىْ بُنَىَّ عَمَّنْ أَخَذْتَ هَذَا قُلْتُ عَنْكَ . قَالَ إِنَّ رَسُولَ اللهِ صَلَّى اللهُ عَلَيْهِ وَسَلَّمَ كَانَ يَقُولُهُنَّ فِي دُبُرِ الصَّلاَةِ .

"My father (radiallahu anhu) used to say at the end of the prayer: 'O Allah, I seek refuge in you from disbelief, poverty, and the punishment of the grave.' So I used to say them too. Then my father asked me, 'Oh my son, from whom did you get this?' I said, 'From you.' Then he said, 'Indeed, the Messenger of Allah used to say them at the end of the prayer.'" [61]

50. It is related that Umar bin Al-Khatab (radiallahu anhu) said:

كَانَ النَّبِيُّ صَلَّى اللهُ عَلَيْهِ ولم يَتَعَوَّذُ مِنْ خَمْسٍ مِنَ الْجُبْنِ وَالْبُخْلِ وَسُوءِ الْعُمْرِ وَفِتْنَةِ الصَّدْرِ وَعَذَابِ الْقَبْرِ .

"The Prophet (sallallahu alaihi wa sallam) used to seek refuge from five: cowardice, miserliness,

[61] Reported by An-Nisaa'i (3/73) and Ahmad (5/36).
Sheikh Al-Albani declared it authentic in "Sahih An-Nisaa'i", number: 1346.

decrepitude, trials of the heart, and the punishment of the grave." [62]

51. It is related that Abdurahman bin Abi Bakra said to his father:

قَالَ لأَبِيهِ يَا أَبَةِ إِنِّي أَسْمَعُكَ تَدْعُو كُلَّ غَدَاةٍ .... ، وَتَقُولُ اللَّهُمَّ إِنِّي أَعُوذُ بِكَ مِنَ الْكُفْرِ وَالْفَقْرِ اللَّهُمَّ إِنِّي أَعُوذُ بِكَ مِنْ عَذَابِ الْقَبْرِ لاَ إِلَهَ إِلاَّ أَنْتَ تُعِيدُهَا ثَلاَثًا حِينَ تُصْبِحُ وَثَلاَثًا حِينَ تُمْسِي فَتَدْعُو بِهِنَّ . فَقَالَ : إِنِّي سَمِعْتُ رَسُولَ اللهِ - صَلَّى اللهُ عَلَيْهِ وَ سَلَّمَ - يَدْعُو بِهِنَّ ، فَأَنَا أُحِبُّ أَنْ أَسْتَنَّ بِسُنَّتِهِ .

"I hear you supplicating every day and you say: 'O Allah, I seek refuge in you from disbelief and poverty. O Allah, I seek refuge in you from the punishment in the grave. There is none worthy except you.' You repeat it three times in the morning

[62] Reported by Abu Dawud, number: 1539; Ibn Majah, number: 3844; and An-Nasa'i in "Al-Kubra", number: 7879, 7915, 7917, 7934, and 9963, and in "As-Sugra", number: 5446.
It has support from the hadith of Ibn Mas'ood, reported by Ahmad, numbers: 145 and 388. Shu'aib declared it authentic to the standard of Al-Bukhari and Muslim, and likewise, Al-Hakim.
Sheikh Al-Albani declared it weak in "Da'if Al-Jami'", number: 4533; "Da'if Abi Dawud", number: 1316; "Da'if Ibn Majah", number: 838; and "Da'if An-Nasaa'i", number: 5480 and 419.

and evening." He said: "I heard the Messenger of Allah (sallallahu alaihi wa sallam) supplicate with it, and I like to follow his sunnah."[63]

52. It is related from A'isha (radiallahu anha), the wife of the Prophet (sallallahu alaihi wa sallam), that the Messenger of Allah used to supplicate to Allah in the prayer, saying:

اللَّهُمَّ إِنِّي أَعُوذُ بِكَ مِنْ عَذَابِ الْقَبْرِ ، وَ أَعُوذُ بِكَ مِنْ فِتْنَةِ الْمَسِيحِ الدَّجَّالِ ، وَ أَعُوذُ بِكَ مِنْ فِتْنَةِ الْمَحْيَى ، وَ فِتْنَةِ الْمَمَاتِ ، اللَّهُمَّ إِنِّي أَعُوذُ بِكَ مِنَ الْمَأْثَمِ وَ الْمَغْرَمِ .

"O Allah, I seek refuge with You from the punishment of the grave and from the trial of the *Masih Ad-Dajjal* and from the trials of life and death. O Allah, I seek refuge with You from the sins and from being in debt."[64]

---

[63] Reported by Abu Dawud, number: 5090; At-Tirmidhi, number: 3503; Ahmad, number: 20,447; and Al-Hakim, number: 1954.
Sheikh Al-Albani (rahimahullah) declared it to be authentic in "Sahih Sunan Abi Dawud", number: 5090.
See: "Al-Irwa" (3/356).

[64] Reported by Al-Bukhari, number: 798; and Muslim, number: 587 and 589.

53. It is related that Anas bin Malik (radiallahu anhu) said that the Messenger of Allah (sallallahu alaihi wa sallam) used to say:

اللَّهُمَّ إِنِّي أَعُوذُ بِكَ مِنَ الْعَجْزِ ، وَ الْكَسَلِ ، وَ الْجُبْنِ ، وَ الْهَرَمِ ، وَ أَعُوذُ بِكَ مِنْ فِتْنَةِ الْمَحْيَى ، وَ الْمَمَاتِ ، وَ أَعُوذُ بِكَ مِنْ عَذَابِ الْقَبْرِ

"O Allah, I seek refuge in you from weakness, laziness, miserliness, cowardice, and decrepitude. I seek refuge in you from the trials of life and death, and I seek refuge in you from the punishment of the grave."[65]

54. It is related that Abdullah bin Mas'ood (radiallahu anhu) said:

كَانَ رَسُولُ اللهِ - صَلَّى اللهُ عَلَيْهِ وَ سَلَّمَ - إِذَا أَمْسَى ، وَ إِذَا أَصْبَحَ ، قَالَ : ((اللَّهُمَّ إِنِّي أَعُوذُ بِكَ مِنْ عَذَابٍ فِي النَّارِ ، وَ عَذَابٍ فِي الْقَبْرِ)) .

"The Messenger of Allah used to say in the morning and evening: 'O Allah, I seek refuge in you from the

[65] Reported by Al-Bukhari, number: 2668; and Muslim, number: 2706.

punishment of the fire and the punishment in the grave.'"[66]

55. It is related that A'ishah said: "The Prophet (sallallahu alaihi wa sallam) used to say:

اللَّهُمَّ إِنِّي أَعُوذُ بِكَ مِنْ فِتْنَةِ الْقَبْرِ ، وَ عَذَابِ الْقَبْرِ ....

'...O Allah, I seek refuge in you from the trial of the grave, and the punishment of the grave...'"[67]

56. It is related that A'ishah said that the Messenger of Allah (sallallahu alaihi wa sallam) said:

اللَّهُمَّ رَبَّ جِبْرَائِيلَ ، وَ مِيكَائِيلَ ، وَ رَبَّ إِسْرَافِيلَ ، أَعُوذُ بِكَ مِنْ حَرِّ النَّارِ ، وَ عَذَابِ الْقَبْرِ .

"O Allah, Lord of Jibril and Mika'il, and the Lord of Israfil, I seek refuge in you from the heat of the hellfire, and the punishment of the grave."[68]

---

[66] Reported by Muslim, number: 2723.
[67] Reported by Al-Bukhari, number: 6014; and Muslim, number: 589.
As it is reported in "Lu'lu' wal Marian", number: 1731.
[68] Reported by An-Nisaa'i (3/72)(1345).
As it is reported in "As-Silsilah As-Sahihah" by Al-Albani, number: 1544.

57. It is reported by Ubay bin Ka'b (radiallahu anhu) that the Messenger of Allah (sallallahu alaihi wa sallam) said:

الدَّجَّالُ عَيْنُهُ خَضْرَاءُ كَالزُّجَاجَةِ ، وَ نَعُوذُ بِاللهِ مِنْ عَذَابِ الْقَبْرِ .

"The *Dajjal's* eye is green like a glass bottle, and we seek refuge in Allah from the punishment of the grave."[69]

58. It is related that Said bin Abi Waqqas (radiallahu anhu) used to teach his children these words, as a teacher teaches a boy how to write, and he would say:

إِنَّ رَسُولَ اللهِ - صَلَّى اللهُ عَلَيْهِ وَ سَلَّمَ - كَانَ يَتَعَوَّذُ مِنْهُنَّ دُبُرَ الصَّلَاةِ : ((اللَّهُمَّ إِنِّي أَعُوذُ بِكَ مِنَ الْجُبْنِ ، وَ أَعُوذُ بِكَ أَنْ أُرَدَّ إِلَى أَرْذَلِ الْعُمُرِ ، وَ أَعُوذُ بِكَ مِنْ فِتْنَةِ الدُّنْيَا ، وَ أَعُوذُ بِكَ مِنْ عَذَابِ الْقَبْرِ)) .

"The Messenger of Allah used to seek refuge from them at the end of the prayer (saying): 'O Allah, I seek refuge in you from cowardice, and I seek refuge in you from returning to a decrepit age, and I

---

[69] Reported by Ahmad and Abu Na'im in "Akhbar Asbahan".
Sheikh Al-Albani said in "As-Silsilah As-Sahihah", number: 1863: "Its chain of narration is authentic and its narrators are trustworthy."

seek refuge in you from the trials of life, and I seek refuge in you from the punishment of the grave.'" [70]

59. It is related from Umm Khalid bint Khalid bin Sa'id bin Al-Aas (radiallahu anha) ,

أَنَّهَا سَمِعَتِ النَّبِيَّ - صَلَّى اللهُ عَلَيْهِ وَ سَلَّمَ - وَ هُوَ يَتَعَوَّذُ مِنْ عَذَابِ الْقَبْرِ .

that she heard the Prophet (sallallahu alaihi wa sallam) seek refuge from the punishment of the grave.[71]

60. It is related that Abu Hurairah said that the Messenger of Allah said:

اللَّهُمَّ إِنِّي أَعُوذُ بِكَ مِنْ عَذَابِ الْقَبْرِ ، وَ مِنْ عَذَابِ النَّارِ ، وَ مِنْ فِتْنَةِ الْمَحْيَا وَ الْمَمَاتِ ، وَ مِنْ فِتْنَةِ الْمَسِيحِ الدَّجَّالِ .

"O Allah, I seek refuge in you from the punishment of the grave, the punishment of the fire, the trials of

[70] Reported by Al-Bukhari, number: 2667. See "As-Silsilah As-Sahihah", number: 3937.
[71] Reported by Al-Bukhari, number: 1310.

life and death, and from the trials of the *Masih Ad-Dajjal*."[72]

61. It is related that Jabir bin Abdullah Al-Ansari (radiallahu anhu) said:

دَخَلَ النَّبِيُّ - صَلَّى اللهُ عَلَيْهِ وَ سَلَّمَ - نَخْلًا لِبَنِي النَّجَّارِ ، فَسَمِعَ أَصْوَاتَ رِجَالٍ مِنْ بَنِي النَّجَّارِ ، مَاتُوا فِي الْجَاهِلِيَّةِ ، يُعَذَّبُونَ فِي قُبُورِهِمْ ، فَخَرَجَ رَسُولُ اللهِ - صَلَّى اللهُ عَلَيْهِ وَ سَلَّمَ فَزِعًا ، فَأَمَرَ أَصْحَابَهُ أَنْ يَتَعَوَّذُوا مِنْ عَذَابِ الْقَبْرِ .

"The Prophet entered a garden owned by Bani An-Najjar when he heard the voices of men from Bani An-Najjar, who had died in the time of *Jahiliyah,* being punished in their graves. The Messenger of Allah quickly left in a panic and ordered his companions to seek refuge from the punishment of the grave."[73]

---

[72] Reported by Al-Bukhari, number: 1311; and Muslim, number: 588.
[73] Reported by Abdurazzaq in "Al-Musanaf" and Ahmad in "Al-Musnad" and his book "As-Sunnah".
Sheikh Al-Albani said in "As-Silsilah As-Sahihah", number: 3954: "Its chain of narration is authentic to the standard of Muslim."

62. It is related that Zaid bin Arqam said that the Messenger of Allah (sallallahu alaihi wa sallam) used to say:

اللَّهُمَّ إِنِّي أَعُوذُ بِكَ مِنَ الْعَجْزِ ، وَ الْكَسَلِ ، وَ الْجُبْنِ ، وَ الْهَرَمِ ، وَ عَذَابِ الْقَبْرِ .

"O Allah, I seek refuge in you from weakness, laziness, cowardice, miserliness, decrepitude, and the punishment of the grave."[74]

[74] Reported by Muslim, number: 2722.
See "As-Silsilah As-Sahihah" by Sheikh Al-Albani (rahimahullah), number: 4005.

CHAPTER 7: ANIMALS HEAR THE PEOPLE BEING PUNISHED IN THEIR GRAVES.

63. It is related that Abdullah bin Mas'ood related that the Prophet (sallallahu alaihi wa sallam) said:

إِنَّ الْمَوْتَى لَيُعَذَّبُونَ فِي قُبُورِهِمْ ، حَتَّى إِنَّ الْبَهَائِمَ لَتَسْمَعُ أَصْوَاتَهُمْ

"Verily, the deceased will be punished in their graves to the extent that animals can hear their voices."[75]

64. It is related that Abu Said Al-Khudri (radiallahu anhu) said that the Messenger of Allah said:

إِذَا وُضِعَتِ الْجَنَازَةُ ، فَاحْتَمَلَهَا الرِّجَالُ عَلَى أَعْنَاقِهِمْ ، فَإِنْ كَانَتْ صَالِحَةً ، قَالَتْ : قَدِّمُونِي ، قَدِّمُونِي . وَ إِنْ كَانَتْ غَيْرَ صَالِحَةٍ ، قَالَتْ : يَا وَيْلَهَا ! أَيْنَ يَذْهَبُونَ بِهَا ؟ يَسْمَعُ صَوْتَهَا كُلُّ شَيْءٍ ، إِلَّا الإِنْسَانَ ، وَ لَوْ سَمِعَهَا الإِنْسَانُ ، لَصَعِقَ .

[75] Reported by At-Tabarani in "Al-Kabir".
Sheikh Al-Albani (rahimahullah) said in "Sahih At-Targhib wat Tarhib", number: 3548: "authentic".

"When the funeral is ready and the men carry it on their shoulders, if the deceased was righteous it will say, 'Present me (hurriedly),' and if he was not righteous, it will say, 'Woe to me. Where are they taking me?' Its voice is heard by everything except man, and if he heard it, he would fall unconscious."[76]

65. It is related that Umm Mubashir said

دَخَلَ عَلَيَّ رَسُولُ اللهِ - صَلَّى اللهُ عَلَيْهِ وَ سَلَّمَ - ، وَ أَنَا فِي حَائِطٍ مِنْ حَوَائِطِ بَنِي النَّجَّارِ ، فِيهِ قُبُورٌ مِنْهُمْ ، قَدْ مَاتُوا فِي الْجَاهِلِيَّةِ ، فَسَمِعَهُمْ وَ هُمْ يُعَذَّبُونَ ، فَخَرَجَ ، وَ هُوَ يَقُولُ : ((اسْتَعِيذُوا بِاللهِ مِنْ عَذَابِ الْقَبْرِ)) قَالَتْ : قُلْتُ : يَا رَسُولَ اللهِ ، وَ إِنَّهُمْ لَيُعَذَّبُونَ فِي قُبُورِهِمْ ؟ قَالَ : ((نَعَمْ ، عَذَابًا تَسْمَعُهُ الْبَهَائِمِ)) .

that the Messenger of Allah came to her whilst she was in a garden belonging to Bani An-Najjar, in which there were some of their graves whom had died during *Jahiliyah*. He heard them being punished and so left the garden saying: "Seek refuge in Allah from the punishment of the grave!"

---

[76] Reported by Al-Bukhari, number: 1314.

She said: "I said: 'O Messenger of Allah, are they being tortured in their graves?'" He said: "Yes, a punishment that can be heard by the animals."[77]

---

[77] Reported by Ibn Hibban, number: 787, and Ahmad.
Sheikh Al-Albani in "As-Silsilah As-Sahihah", number 1444, said: "Its chain of narration is authentic to the standard of Muslim."

CHAPTER 8: THE TWO ANGELS QUESTIONING OF THE DECEASED IN THE GRAVE.

66. It is related that Al-Bara bin Azib related that the Prophet (sallallahu alaihi wa sallam) said:

إِذَا أُقْعِدَ الْمُؤْمِنُ فِي قَبْرِهِ، أُتِيَ، ثُمَّ شَهِدَ أَنْ لَا إِلَهَ إِلَّا اللهُ ، وَ أَنَّ مُحَمَّدًا رَسُولُ اللهِ ، فَذَلِكَ قَوْلُهُ : ((يُثَبِّتُ اللهُ الَّذِينَ ءَامَنُوا بِالْقَوْلِ الثَّابِتِ))

"If the believer is laid in his grave, he will testify that none has the right to be worshipped but Allah and that Muhammad is the Messenger of Allah and that is what is meant by Allah's Statement:

'Allah will keep firm those who believe with a Word that stands firm in this world and in the Hereafter.'"[78]

---

[78] Reported by Al-Bukhari, number: 1303; Muslim, number: 2871; and Ibn Hibban, number 206, with the checking done by Al-Albani.
The wording that is reported by Muslim: "Allah will keep firm those who believe with a Word that stands firm in this world and in the Hereafter." This was revealed concerning the punishment of the grave, so it will be said to him "Who is your Lord?" So he will say: "My Lord is Allah and my Prophet is Muhammad." So that is the meaning of Allah's statement:

67. It is related that Abu Hurairah said that the Messenger of Allah said:

إِذَا قُبِرَ الْمَيِّتُ - أَوْ قَالَ : أَحَدُكُمْ - أَتَاهُ مَلَكَانِ ، أَسْوَدَانِ ، أَزْرَقَانِ ، يُقَالُ لِأَحَدِهِمَا : الْمُنْكَرُ . وَالْآخَرُ : النَّكِيرُ . فَيَقُولَانِ : مَا كُنْتَ تَقُولُ فِي هَذَا الرَّجُلِ ؟ فَيَقُولُ مَا كَانَ يَقُولُ : هُوَ عَبْدُ اللهِ ، وَ رَسُولُهُ ، أَشْهَدُ أَنْ لَا إِلَهَ إِلَّا اللهُ ، وَ مُحَمَّدًا عَبْدُهُ وَ رَسُولُهُ . فَيَقُولَانِ : قَدْ كُنَّا نَعْلَمُ أَنَّكَ تَقُولُ هَذَا . ثُمَّ يُفْسَحُ لَهُ فِي قَبْرِهِ ، سَبْعُونَ ذِرَاعًا فِي سَبْعِينَ ، ثُمَّ يُنَوَّرُ لَهُ فِيهِ ، ثُمَّ يُقَالُ لَهُ : نَمْ . فَيَقُولُ : أَرْجِعُ إِلَى أَهْلِي ، فَأُخْبِرُهُمْ . فَيَقُولَانِ : نَمْ كَنَوْمَةِ الْعَرُوسِ ، الَّذِي لَا يُوقِظُهُ إِلَّا أَحَبُّ أَهْلِهِ إِلَيْهِ ، حَتَّى يَبْعَثَهُ اللهُ مِنْ مَضْجَعِهِ ذَلِكَ .

وَ إِنْ كَانَ مُنَافِقًا ، قَالَ : سَمِعْتُ النَّاسَ يَقُولُونَ ، فَقُلْتُ مِثْلَهُ ، لَا أَدْرِي . فَيَقُولَانِ : قَدْ كُنَّا نَعْلَمُ أَنَّكَ

"Allah will keep firm those who believe with a Word that stands firm in this world and in the Hereafter."
See "Silsilah As-Sahihah" by Al-Albani, number: 3963.

تَقُولُ ذَلِكَ . فَيُقَالُ لِلْأَرْضِ : الْتَئِمِي عَلَيْهِ . فَتَلْتَئِمُ عَلَيْهِ ، فَتَخْتَلِفُ فِيهَا أَضْلَاعُهُ ، فَيَزَالُ فِيهَا مُعَذَّبًا ، حَتَّى يَبْعَثَهُ اللهُ مِنْ مَضْجَعِهِ ذَلِكَ .

“If the deceased (or any of you) is buried, two angels, black and blue, come to him; one called Al-Munkar and the other called An-Nakir. They will say: 'What did you used to say about this man?' So he will say what he used to say: 'He is Allah's slave and His messenger. I bear witness that there is none worthy of worship except Allah, and that Muhammad is His slave and messenger.' Then they will say: 'We knew you would say this.' Then his grave will be expanded to seventy by seventy cubits and his grave will be lit up for him, and it will be said: 'Sleep.' He will say: 'Let me return to my family so I can inform them.' The Angels will say: 'Go to sleep like the newlywed that none will awaken except the most beloved of his family;' until Allah will resurrect him from that resting place.

“If he was a hypocrite, he will say: 'I used to hear the people saying something, so I said the same, I do not know.' They will say: 'We knew you would say that.' So the earth is told: 'Constrict him.' So it constricts around him, squeezing his ribs together.

He continues being punished like that until Allah resurrects him from that resting place."[79]

68. It is related that Anas bin Malik (radiallahu anhu) said that the Messenger of Allah (sallallahu alaihi wa sallam) said:

إِنَّ الْعَبْدَ إِذَا وُضِعَ فِي قَبْرِهِ، وَتَوَلَّى عَنْهُ أَصْحَابُهُ، وَإِنَّهُ لَيَسْمَعُ قَرْعَ نِعَالِهِمْ، أَتَاهُ مَلَكَانِ فَيُقْعِدَانِهِ فَيَقُولاَنِ مَا كُنْتَ تَقُولُ فِي الرَّجُلِ لِمُحَمَّدٍ صَلَّى اللهُ عَلَيْهِ وَسَلَّمَ. فَأَمَّا الْمُؤْمِنُ فَيَقُولُ أَشْهَدُ أَنَّهُ عَبْدُ اللهِ وَرَسُولُهُ. فَيُقَالُ لَهُ انْظُرْ إِلَى مَقْعَدِكَ مِنَ النَّارِ، قَدْ أَبْدَلَكَ اللهُ بِهِ مَقْعَدًا مِنَ الْجَنَّةِ، فَيَرَاهُمَا جَمِيعًا . قَالَ قَتَادَةُ وَذُكِرَ لَنَا أَنَّهُ يُفْسَحُ فِي قَبْرِهِ. ثُمَّ رَجَعَ إِلَى حَدِيثِ أَنَسٍ قَالَ : ((وَأَمَّا الْمُنَافِقُ وَالْكَافِرُ فَيُقَالُ لَهُ مَا كُنْتَ تَقُولُ فِي هَذَا الرَّجُلِ فَيَقُولُ لاَ أَدْرِي، كُنْتُ أَقُولُ مَا يَقُولُ النَّاسُ. فَيُقَالُ لاَ دَرَيْتَ وَلاَ تَلَيْتَ. وَيُضْرَبُ بِمَطَارِقَ مِنْ

[79] Reported by At-Tirmidhi, and Ibn Abi Aasim in "As-Sunnah", number: 864, with a checking by Al-Albani.
Sheikh Al-Albani declared its chain of narration to be good, and he said: "Its narrators are all trustworthy and are narrators of Imam Muslim."
As reported in "As-Silsilah As-Sahihah", number: 1391.

حَدِيدٍ ضَرْبَةً، فَيَصِيحُ صَيْحَةً يَسْمَعُهَا مَنْ يَلِيهِ، غَيْرَ الثَّقَلَيْنِ)) .

"When the slave is placed in his grave and his companions leave, he hears their footsteps, and then two angels come to him and make him sit up and ask, 'What did you use to say about this man (i.e., Muhammad [sallallahu alaihi wa sallam])?' The believer will say, 'I bear witness that he is Allah's slave and His messenger.' Then they will say to him, 'Look at your place in the Hell Fire; Allah has replaced it with a place in Paradise.' So he will see both his places. (Qatada said: 'We were told that his grave would be expanded to seventy cubits and it would be filled with greenery until the day he is resurrected.') As for a hypocrite or a non-believer, he will be asked, 'What did you use to say about this man?' He will reply: 'I do not know; I used to say what the people used to say.' So they will say to him: 'Neither did you know nor did you recite (the Quran).' Then he will be hit with an iron hammer, so he will cry out so loud that everything near him will hear, except Jinns and human beings." [80]

69. It is related from Abdullah bin Amr bin Al-Aas (radiallahu anhu) that the Messenger of Allah (sallallahu

---

[80] Reported by Al-Bukhari, number: 1308; and Muslim, number: 2870. As reported in "Sahih At-Targheeb wat Tarheeb", number: 3555.

alaihi wa sallam) mentioned the trial of the grave, so Umar said:

أَ تَرِدُّ عَلَيْنَا عُقُولُنَا يَا رَسُولَ اللهِ ؟ ! فَقَالَ رَسُولُ اللهِ - صَلَّى اللهُ عَلَيْهِ وَ سَلَّمَ : ((نَعَمْ ، كَهَيْئَتِكَ الْيَوْمَ)) .

"Will our consciousness be returned to us, O Messenger of Allah?" The Messenger of Allah (sallallahu alaihi wa sallam) said: "Yes, like your appearance today."[81]

70. It is related that Asma bint Abu Bakr As-Siddiq (radiallahu anha) related that the Messenger of Allah stood to address the people, so he praised Allah and commended Him, then he said:

أَمَّا بَعْدُ : مَا مِنْ شَيْءٍ لَمْ أَكُنْ رَأَيْتُهُ ، إِلَّا قَدْ رَأَيْتُهُ فِي مَقَامِي هَذَا ، حَتَّى الْجَنَّةَ وَ النَّارَ ، وَ إِنَّهُ قَدْ أُوحِيَ إِلَيَّ أَنَّكُمْ تُفْتَنُونَ فِي الْقُبُورِ قَرِيبًا أَوْ مِثْلَ فِتْنَةِ الْمَسِيحِ الدَّجَّالِ . فَلَمَّا ذَكَرَ ذَلِكَ ضَجَّ الْمُسْلِمُونَ ضَجَّةً ، قَالَ : ((فَيُؤْتَى أَحَدُكُمْ ، فَيُقَالُ : مَا عِلْمُكُمْ بِهَذَا الرَّجُلِ ؟ فَأَمَّا الْمُؤْمِنُ أَوِ الْمُوقِنُ - لَا أَدْرِي أَيَّ

[81] Reported by Ahmad, and At-Tabarani. Sheikh Al-Albani (rahimahullah) declared it "good" in "Sahih At-Targhib wat Tarhib", number: 3553. Al-Mundhari declared its chain of narration to be "good."

ذَلِكَ قَالَتْ أَسْمَاءُ - فَيَقُولُ : هُوَ مُحَمَّدٌ رَسُولُ اللهِ ، جَاءَنَا بِالْبَيِّنَاتِ وَ الْهُدَى ، فَأَجَبْنَا ، وَ أَطَعْنَا ، وَ اتَّبَعْنَا (ثَلَاثَ مَرَّاتٍ) . فَيُقَالُ لَهُ : نَمْ ، قَدْ كُنَّا نَعْلَمُ إِنَّكَ لَتُؤْمِنُ بِهِ ، فَنَمْ صَالِحًا .

وَ أَمَّا الْمُنَافِقُ أَوِ الْمُرْتَابُ - لَا أَدْرِي أَيَّ ذَلِكَ قَالَتْ أَسْمَاءُ - فَيَقُولُ : لَا أَدْرِي ، سَمِعْتُ النَّاسَ يَقُولُونَ شَيْئًا ، فَقُلْتُ))

"I have seen at this place of mine what I have never seen, even Paradise and Hell. It has been revealed to me that you will be put to trial in the graves like the trial of *Al-Masih Ad-Dajjal*." When he mentioned that, the Muslims began to make noise, and he said: "Each one of you would be brought and it would be said: 'What is your knowledge about this man?' The believer or the person that is certain would say: 'He is Muhammad and he is the Messenger of Allah. He brought to us the clear signs and right guidance. So we responded, obeyed him and followed him.' (Three times), and it would be said to him: 'You should go to sleep. We already knew that you are a believer in him, so sleep righteously.'"

As for where the hypocrite or sceptic is concerned (Asma' said: 'I do not know which') he would say: 'I

do not know. I only uttered whatever I heard people say.'[82]

71. It is related that Uthman bin Affan said that when the Prophet (sallallahu alaihi wa sallam) used to finish burying the deceased, he would stop and say:

اسْتَغْفِرُوا لِأَخِيكُمْ ، وَاسْأَلُوا لَهُ التَّثْبِيتَ ، فَإِنَّهُ الْآنَ يُسْأَلُ .

"Seek forgiveness for your brother and ask for him to be firm, as he is now being questioned."[83]

72. It is related from A'ishah[84] (radiallahu anha) that she said:

---

[82] Reported by Al-Bukhari, number: 86 and 1307; and Muslim, number: 905.

[83] Reported by Abu Dawud, number: 3221; and Al-Hakim (1/370)(1372). Al-Hakim declared it authentic and Adh-Dhahabi agreed. Shuaib Al-Arna'oot declared it to be good in his comments on "Riyadh As-Salihin." Sheikh Muqbil (rahimahullah) also declared it to be good in "Al-Jami' As-Sahih mima Laissa fis Sahihain" (2/263). Sheikh Al-Albani (rahimahullah) declared it to be authentic, number: 956.

[84] Reported by Al-Bazzar. Sheikh Al-Albani (rahimahullah) said in "Sahih At-Targhib wat Tarhib", number 3554: "authentic due to supporting narrations." And Al-Mundhari said: "Its narrators are trustworthy."

قُلْتُ يَا رَسُولَ اللهِ ، تَبْتَلَى هَذِهِ الْأُمَّةُ فِي قُبُورِهَا ، فَكَيْفَ بِي ، وَ أَنَا امْرَأَةٌ ضَعِيفَةٌ ؟ قَالَ : ﴿ يُثَبِّتُ ٱللَّهُ ٱلَّذِينَ ءَامَنُوا۟ بِٱلْقَوْلِ ٱلثَّابِتِ فِى ٱلْحَيَوٰةِ ٱلدُّنْيَا وَفِى ٱلْءَاخِرَةِ ﴾

"I said: 'O Messenger of Allah, this Ummah will be tested in their graves, so what about me: I'm just a weak woman?' So he said: 'Allah will keep firm those who believe, with the word that stands firm in this world, and in the Hereafter.'"[85]

74. It is related that Abu Sa'id Al-Khudri (radiallahu anhu) said:

شَهِدْتُ مَعَ رَسُولِ اللهِ - صَلَّى اللهُ عَلَيْهِ وَ سَلَّمَ - جِنَازَةً ، فَقَالَ رَسُولُ اللهِ - صَلَّى اللهُ عَلَيْهِ وَ سَلَّمَ : ((يَا أَيُّهَا النَّاسُ ، إِنَّ هَذِهِ الْأُمَّةَ تَبْتَلَى فِي قُبُورِهَا ، فَإِذَا الْإِنْسَانُ دُفِنَ ، فَتَفَرَّقَ عَنْهُ أَصْحَابُهُ ، جَاءَهُ مَلَكٌ فِي يَدِهِ مِطْرَاقٌ ، فَأَقْعَدَهُ ، قَالَ : مَا تَقُولُ فِي هَذَا الرَّجُلِ ؟ ... وَ يُفْسَحُ لَهُ فِي قَبْرِهِ ....))

"I attended a funeral with the Messenger of Allah (sallallahu alaihi wa sallam), then the Messenger of

[85] (Ibrahim: 27).

Allah (sallallahu alaihi wa sallam) said: 'O people, this nation will be tested in their graves, so when a person is buried, and his companions leave, an angel comes to him with a hammer in its hand and makes him sit up and says: 'What do you say about this man?'...and expands his grave...'"[86]

[86] Reported by Ahmad, Ibn Jarir in "At-Tafsir", Ibn Abi Aasim in "As-Sunnah", and Al-Bazzar. Sheikh Al-Albani declared it authentic in "As-Silsilah As-Sahihah", number: 3394.

CHAPTER 9: WHO WILL NOT BE QUESTIONED IN HIS GRAVE?

75. It is related from a companion of the Prophet (sallallahu alaihi wa sallam) that a man said:

يَا رَسُولَ اللهِ ، مَا بَالُ الْمُؤْمِنِينَ يُفْتَنُونَ فِي قُبُورِهِمْ ، إِلَّا الشَّهِيدَ ؟! قَالَ : ((كَفَى بِبَارِقَةِ السُّيُوفِ عَلَى رَأْسِهِ فِتْنَةً)) .

"O Messenger of Allah, why are the believers tested in their graves but not the martyr?!" He said: "It is enough of a test to be struck on the head with a sword."[87]

76. It is related that Salman Al-Farisi (radiallahu anhu) said that the Messenger of Allah (sallallahu alaihi wa sallam) said:

رِبَاطُ يَوْمٍ وَ لَيْلَةٍ خَيْرٌ مِنْ صِيَامِ شَهْرٍ وَ قِيَامِهِ ، وَ إِنْ مَاتَ جَرَى عَلَيْهِ عَمَلُهُ الَّذِي كَانَ يَعْمَلُهُ ، وَ أُجْرِيَ عَلَيْهِ رِزْقُهُ ، وَ أَمِنَ الْفَتَّانَ .

[87] Reported by An-Nisaa'i (1/289); and it is related from As-Sarqasti in "Gharib Al-Hadith." Sheikh Al-Albani (rahimahullah) declared it to be authentic in "Ahkam Al-Jan'iz", page 50; and in "Sahih Sunan An-Nisaa'i", number: 1940.

"Keeping watch for a day and a night is better than a month of fasting and night prayers. If a person dies (doing that) his activity will continue and he will go on receiving his reward for it perpetually, and he will be saved from the torture of the grave."[88]

77. It is related that Fadalah bin Abeed (radiallahu anhu) said that the Messenger of Allah said:

كُلُّ مَيِّتٍ يُخْتَمُ عَلَى عَمَلِهِ ، إِلَّا الَّذِي مَاتَ مُرَابِطًا فِي سَبِيلِ اللهِ ، فَإِنَّهُ يُنَمَّى لَهث عَمَلُهُ إِلَى يَوْمِ الْقِيَامَةِ، وَ يَأْمَنُ فِتْنَةَ الْقَبْرِ

"The actions of every deceased are concluded, except the one who died keeping watch for the sake of Allah, for indeed his actions will continue to grow till the Day of Resurrection, and he is saved from the punishment of the grave." [89]

---

[88] Reported by Muslim, number: 1913. See: "Ahkam Al-Jana'iz" by Al-Albani (rahimahullah), page: 58.

[89] Reported by Ahmad, Abu Dawud, At-Tirmidhi, and Al-Hakim. At-Tirmidhi and Al-Hakim declared it authentic, reported as it was in "Ahkam Al-Jana'iz", page: 58. Sheikh Muqbil Al-Wadi'i declared it authentic in "Al-Musnad As-Sahih" (2/152), and "Al-Jami' As-Sahih" (2/277).

78. It is related that Abdullah bin Amr Al-Aas (radiallahu anhu) said that the Messenger of Allah said:

مَا مِنْ مُسْلِمٍ يَمُوتُ يَوْمَ الْجُمْعَةِ ، أَوْ لَيْلَةَ الْجُمْعَةِ ، إِلَّا وَقَاهُ اللهُ فِتْنَةَ الْقَبْرِ .

"Any Muslim that dies on the day or night of Jumuah will be protected by Allah from the trial of the grave."[90]

79. It is related that Abdullah bin Yasar said:

كُنْتُ جَالِسًا ، وَ سُلَيْمَانُ بْنُ صُرَدٍ ، وَ خَالِدُ بْنُ عُرْفُطَةَ ، فَذَكَرُوا أَنَّ رَجُلًا تُوُفِّيَ ، مَاتَ بِبَطْنِهِ ، وَ إِذَا هُمَا يَشْتَهِيَانِ أَنْ يَكُونَا شُهَدَاءَ جَنَازَتِهِ ، فَقَالَ الْآخَرُ : بَلَى .

"I was sitting with Sulaiman bin Sard and Khalid bin Urfutah, and they said that a man had died due to an abdominal illness. They wanted to attend his funeral, and one of them said to the other: 'Didn't the Messenger of Allah say: 'Whoever is killed by

[90] Reported by Ahmad, number: 6582 and 6646; and Al-Faswi in "Al-Ma'rifa". As it is reported in "Ahkam Al-Jana'iz" by Al-Albani (rahimahullah), pages: 49-50, and in "Sahih At-Targhib wat Tarhib", number: 3562.

an abdominal illness, he will not be punished in his grave?" The other said: 'Yes.'"[91]

ꕥ ✹ ✹ ✹ ꕥ

[91] Reported by At-Tiyaalisi, number: 1288; Ahmad, At-Tirmidhi, An-Nasa'i, and Ibn Hibban. Sheikh Al-Albani (rahimahullah) declared it authentic in "Ahkam Al-Jana'iz".

CHAPTER 10: NARROWING OF THE GRAVE

80. It is related that Abdullah bin Umar (radiallahu anhu) said that the Messenger of Allah (sallallahu alaihi wa sallam) said:

لَقَدْ نَزَلَ لِمَوْتِ سَعْدِ بْنِ مُعَاذٍ سَبْعُونَ أَلْفَ مَلَكٍ ، مَا وَطِئُوا الْأَرْضَ قَبْلَهَا . وَ قَالَ حِينَ دُفِنَ : ((سُبْحَانَ اللهِ ، لَوِ انْفَلَتَ أَحَدٌ مِنْ ضَغْطَةِ الْقَبْرِ ، لَانْفَلَتَ مِنْهَا سَعْدٌ ، وَ لَقَدْ ضُمَّ ضَمَّةً ، ثُمَّ أُفْرِجَ عَنْهُ .

"Seventy thousand angels that had never placed foot on earth before, came down for the death of Sa'ad bin Muadh.

"And he said when he was buried: 'Glorified is Allah! If anyone was to be pardoned from the narrowing of the grave it would be Sa'ad, and indeed he was squeezed once and then released.'"[92]

81. It is related that A'ishah (radiallahu anha) said that the Messenger of Allah (sallallahu alaihi wa sallam) said:

---

[92] Reported by Al-Bazzar. Sheikh Al-Albani declared it to be good in "As-Silsilah As-Sahihah", number: 3345.

إِنَّ لِلْقَبْرِ ضَغْطَةً ، فَلَوْ نَجَا ، أَوْ سَلِمَ أَحَدٌ مِنْهَا ،
لَنَجَا مِنْهَا سَعْدُ بْنُ مُعَاذٍ

"Indeed, the grave is constricting; if anyone were to be saved or safe from it, it would be Sa'ad bin Muadh."[93]

82. It is related by Abu Ayub Al-Ansari (radiallahu anhu) that a child was buried and the Messenger of Allah (sallallahu alaihi wa sallam) said:

لَوْ أُفْلِتَ أَحَدٌ مِنْ ضَمَّةِ الْقَبْرِ ، لَأُفْلِتَ هَذَا الصَّبِيُّ .

"If anyone was to be relieved from the narrowing of the grave, it would be this boy."[94]

---

[93] Reported by Al-Baghawi in "the Hadith of Ali bin Al-Ja'd", and At-Tahawi in "Al-Mushkil". As it is reported in "As-Silsilah As-Sahihah" by Al-Albani, number: 1695.

[94] Reported by At-Tabarani in "Al-Kabir". As it is reported in "As-Silsilah As-Sahihah", number: 2164; Al-Albani's title for it was: "The Narrowing of the Grave: Not even the Child is Saved from it".

CHAPTER 11: THE DECEASED ASK EACH OTHER ABOUT PERSONAL ISSUES

83. It is related from Abu Hurairah (radiallahu anhu) that the Prophet (sallallahu alaihi wa sallam) said:

إِذَا حُضِرَ الْمُؤْمِنُ أَتَتْهُ مَلائِكَةُ الرَّحْمَةِ بِحَرِيرَةٍ بَيْضَاءَ
فَيَقُولُونَ اخْرُجِي رَاضِيَةً مَرْضِيًّا عَنْكِ إِلَى رَوْحِ اللهِ وَرَيْحَانٍ
وَرَبٍّ غَيْرِ غَضْبَانَ . فَتَخْرُجُ كَأَطْيَبِ رِيحِ الْمِسْكِ حَتَّى أَنَّهُ
لَيُنَاوِلُهُ بَعْضُهُمْ بَعْضًا حَتَّى يَأْتُونَ بِهِ بَابَ السَّمَاءِ فَيَقُولُونَ
مَا أَطْيَبَ هَذِهِ الرِّيحَ الَّتِي جَاءَتْكُمْ مِنَ الأَرْضِ . فَيَأْتُونَ بِهِ
أَرْوَاحَ الْمُؤْمِنِينَ فَلَهُمْ أَشَدُّ فَرَحًا بِهِ مِنْ أَحَدِكُمْ بِغَائِبِهِ يَقْدَمُ
عَلَيْهِ فَيَسْأَلُونَهُ مَاذَا فَعَلَ فُلاَنٌ مَاذَا فَعَلَ فُلاَنٌ فَيَقُولُونَ
دَعُوهُ فَإِنَّهُ كَانَ فِي غَمِّ الدُّنْيَا فَإِذَا قَالَ أَمَا أَتَاكُمْ قَالُوا ذُهِبَ
بِهِ إِلَى أُمِّهِ الْهَاوِيَةِ وَإِنَّ الْكَافِرَ إِذَا احْتُضِرَ أَتَتْهُ مَلائِكَةُ
الْعَذَابِ بِمِسْحٍ فَيَقُولُونَ اخْرُجِي سَاخِطَةً مَسْخُوطًا عَلَيْكِ
إِلَى عَذَابِ اللهِ عَزَّ وَجَلَّ . فَتَخْرُجُ كَأَنْتَنِ رِيحِ جِيفَةٍ حَتَّى
يَأْتُونَ بِهِ بَابَ الأَرْضِ فَيَقُولُونَ مَا أَنْتَنَ هَذِهِ الرِّيحَ حَتَّى
يَأْتُونَ بِهِ أَرْوَاحَ الْكُفَّارِ .

"When the believer is dying, the angels of mercy come to him with white silk and say: 'Come out happy, and with Allah's pleasure upon you, to the mercy of Allah, blessings and a Lord Who is not angry.' So the soul comes out like the best fragrance of musk. They pass him from one to another until they bring him to the gate of heaven, where they say: 'How good is this fragrance that has come to you from the Earth!' Then the souls of the believers come to him and they rejoice more over him than any one of you rejoices when his absent loved one comes to him. They ask him: 'What happened to so-and-so? What happened to so-and-so?' They say: 'Let him be, for he was in the hardship of the world.' When he says, 'Did he not come here?' They say: 'He was taken to the pit (of Hell).'

"When the disbeliever is dying, the angels of punishment come with a rough cloth and say: 'Come out embittered, and with Allah's disappointment upon you, to the punishment of Allah, the Mighty and Sublime.' So it comes out like the foulest stench of a corpse. They bring him to the gates of the Earth, where they say: 'How foul is this stench!' Then they bring him to the souls of the disbelievers."[95]

---

[95] Reported by Ibn Majah (2/1423) (4262); Ahmad (3/364) (8754); An-Nisaa'i; Ibn Hibban, number: 733; Al-Bayhaqi in "Ash-Sha'ab" (6/443) (1442); and Al-Hakim. Al-Hakim said: "Its chain of narration is authentic." and Adh-Dhahabi agreed. Sheikh Al-Albani (rahimahullah) said in "As-Silsilah As-Sahihah", number 1309: "It's as he said."

84. It is related from Abu Hurairah that the Messenger of Allah (sallallahu alaihi wa sallam) said:

إِنَّ الْمُؤْمِنَ يَنْزِلُ بِهِ الْمَوْتُ ، وَيُعَايِنُ مَا يُعَايِنُ ، فَوَدَّ لَوْ خَرَجَتْ يَعْنِي : نَفْسَهُ وَاللهُ يُحِبُّ لِقَاءَهُ ، وَإِنَّ الْمُؤْمِنَ يُصْعَدُ بِرُوحِهِ إِلَى السَّمَاءِ ، فَتَأْتِيهِ أَرْوَاحُ الْمُؤْمِنِينَ فَيَسْتَخْبِرُونَهُ عَنْ مَعَارِفِهِمْ مِنْ أَهْلِ الأَرْضِ ، فَإِذَا قَالَ : تَرَكْتُ فُلانًا فِي الدُّنْيَا ، أَعْجَبَهُمْ ذَلِكَ ، وَإِذَا قَالَ : إِنَّ فُلانًا قَدْ مَاتَ ، قَالُوا : مَا جِيءَ بِهِ إِلَيْنَا ، وَإِنَّ الْمُؤْمِنَ يُجْلَسُ فِي قَبْرِهِ ، فَيُسْأَلُ مَنْ رَبُّهُ ، فَيَقُولُ : رَبِّي اللهُ ، فَيَقُولُ : مَنْ نَبِيُّكَ ؟ فَيَقُولُ : نَبِيِّي مُحَمَّدٌ صَلَّى اللهُ عَلَيْهِ وَسَلَّمَ ، قَالَ : فَمَا دِينُكَ ؟ قَالَ : دِينِي الإِسْلامُ ، فَيُفْتَحُ لَهُ بَابٌ فِي قَبْرِهِ ، فَيَقُولُ أَوْ يُقَالُ : انْظُرْ إِلَى مَجْلِسِكَ ، ثُمَّ يُرَى الْقَبْرَ ، فَكَأَنَّمَا كَانَتْ رَقْدَةً ، فَإِذَا كَانَ عَدُوُّ اللهِ نَزَلَ بِهِ الْمَوْتُ ، وَعَايَنَ مَا عَايَنَ ، فَإِنَّهُ لا يُحِبُّ أَنْ تَخْرُجَ رُوحُهُ أَبَدًا ، وَاللهُ يُبْغِضُ لِقَاءَهُ ، فَإِذَا جَلَسَ فِي قَبْرِهِ أَوْ أُجْلِسَ يُقَالُ لَهُ : مَنْ رَبُّكَ ؟ فَيَقُولُ : لا أَدْرِي ، فَيُقَالُ : لا دَرَيْتَ ، فَيُفْتَحُ لَهُ بَابٌ مِنْ جَهَنَّمَ ، ثُمَّ يُضْرَبُ ضَرْبَةً يَسْمَعُ كُلُّ دَابَّةٍ إِلا الثَّقَلَيْنِ ، ثُمَّ يُقَالُ لَهُ : نَمْ كَمَا يَنَامُ الْمَنْهُوشُ

"When death descends upon the believer and he experiences the suffering of that, it wishes it could escape, i.e., his soul, and Allah loves to meet him. The believer's soul is risen up to heaven and the souls of the believers will approach him and ask him about those that they know of the people of Earth. So he, if he says: 'I left so and so behind in the World,' they will become amazed. If he says: 'So and so died,' they will say: 'He wasn't brought to us.'

"And the believer will be made to sit in his grave and will be asked: 'Who is your Lord?' So he will say: 'My Lord is Allah.' Then it will be said to him: 'Who is your prophet?' So he will say: 'My prophet is Muhammad (sallallahu alaihi wa sallam).' He will say: 'What is your religion?' He says: 'My religion is Islam.' A door is opened for him in his grave, and he says, or it is said: 'Look at your resting place.' Then he will be shown his grave and it will be like a large bed.

"When death descends upon the enemy of Allah and he experiences the suffering of that, he wishes that his soul would never leave, and Allah is angered by their meeting. So when he sits in his grave (or is made to sit) and it is said to him: 'Who is your Lord?', and he will say: 'I don't know.' It will be said to him: 'You didn't know.' Then a door to Hell will be opened for him, and he will be struck with a strike that can be heard by the animals. Then it will be said to him: 'Sleep the sleep of the ***manhoosh*** **(something mangled)...'" So I said to Abu**

Hurairah: "What's *manhoosh*?" He said: "Something that has been mangled by animals and snakes...Then his grave tightens around him."[96]

85. It is related that Abu Ayub Al-Ansari said (radiallahu anhu):

إِذَا قُبِضَتْ نَفْسُ الْعَبْدِ تَلَقَّاهُ أَهْلُ الرَّحْمَةِ مِنْ عِبَادِ اللهِ كَمَا يَلْقَوْنَ الْبَشِيرَ فِي الدُّنْيَا ، فَيُقْبِلُونَ عَلَيْهِ لِيَسْأَلُوهُ ، فَيَقُولُ بَعْضُهُمْ لِبَعْضٍ : أَنْظِرُوا أَخَاكُمْ حَتَّى يَسْتَرِيحَ ، فَإِنَّهُ كَانَ فِي كَرْبٍ ، فَيُقْبِلُونَ عَلَيْهِ فَيَسْأَلُونَهُ مَا فَعَلَ فُلانٌ ؟ مَا فَعَلَتْ فُلانَةٌ ؟ هَلْ تَزَوَّجَتْ ؟ فَإِذَا سَأَلُوا عَنِ الرَّجُلِ قَدْ مَاتَ قَبْلَهُ ، قَالَ لَهُمْ : إِنَّهُ قَدْ هَلَكَ ، فَيَقُولُونَ : إِنَّا لِلهِ وَإِنَّا إِلَيْهِ رَاجِعُونَ ذُهِبَ بِهِ إِلَى أُمِّهِ الْهَاوِيَةِ ، فَبِئْسَتِ الأُمُّ ، وَبِئْسَتِ الْمُرَبِّيَةُ ، قَالَ : فَيُعْرَضُ عَلَيْهِمْ أَعْمَالُهُمْ ، فَإِذَا رَأَوْا حَسَنًا فَرِحُوا وَاسْتَبْشَرُوا ، وَقَالُوا : هَذِهِ نِعْمَتُكَ عَلَى عَبْدِكَ فَأَتِمَّهَا ، وَإِنْ رَأَوْا سُوءًا قَالُوا : اللَّهُمَّ رَاجِعْ بِعَبْدِكَ

"When the soul of the slave is removed, he meets the people of mercy from amongst the slaves of Allah, like they would meet the bringer of good news in

---

[96] Reported by Al-Bazzar. As it is reported in "As-Silsilah As-Sahihah" by Al-Albani, number: 2628.

the dunya. So they approach him to ask him: 'What is so and so doing?' and 'What is so and so doing? Did she marry?' If they ask about someone who died before him, he will say: 'He died.' then they will say: 'Everything is for Allah and to him everything will return! He must have been taken to the Hellfire. What a terrible return, what a terrible custodian!' Then they are shown their actions. If they see they are good, they become joyous and rejoice, and they say: 'These are your blessings upon your slave, may You complete it.' But if they see (their actions are) bad, then they say: 'O Allah, may You reassess your slave.'"[97]

86. It is related from Jabir bin Abdullah (radiallahu anhu) that the Messenger of Allah said:

حَدِّثُوا عَنْ بَنِي إِسْرَائِيلَ فَإِنَّهُ كَانَتْ فِيهِمُ الأَعَاجِيبُ وَأَنْشَأَ
رَسُولُ اللهِ صَلَّى اللهُ عَلَيْهِ وَسَلَّمَ ، يُحَدِّثُ ، قَالَ : خَرَجَتْ
طَائِفَةٌ مِنْ بَنِي إِسْرَائِيلَ حَتَّى أَتَوْا مَقْبَرَةً مِنْ مَقَابِرِهِمْ

---

[97] Reported by Ibn Al-Mubarak in "Az-Zuhud". Sheikh Al-Albani (rahimahullah) declared it authentic in "As-Silsilah As-Sahihah", number: 2758, and he said: "It being cut off (i.e., not directly related from the Prophet Muhammad) does not affect it (i.e., its authenticity), as it is about the unseen affairs, which is not possible to be said from opinion, so it has the same ruling as a hadith that is attributed to the Prophet (sallallahu alaihi wa sallam) with certainty, especially since it was also related from the Prophet (via other narrations)."

فَقَالُوا : لَوْ صَلَّيْنَا وَدَعَوْنَا اللهَ عَزَّ وَجَلَّ يُخْرِجُ لَنَا رَجُلا مِمَّنْ قَدْ مَاتَ ، فَنُسَائِلَهُ عَنِ الْمَوْتِ فَفَعَلُوا ، فَبَيْنَاهُمْ كَذَلِكَ إِذْ طَلَعَ رَجُلٌ رَأْسَهُ مِنْ قَبْرٍ مِنْ تِلْكَ الْمَقَابِرِ خُلاسِيٌّ بَيْنَ عَيْنَيْهِ أَثَرُ السُّجُودِ ، فَقَالَ : يَا هَؤُلاءِ ، مَا أَرَدْتُمْ إِلَيَّ لَقَدْ مُتُّ مِنْ مِائَةِ عَامٍ ، فَمَا سَكَتَ عَنِّي حَرَارَةُ الْمَوْتِ إِلا الآنَ ، فَادْعُوا اللهَ عَزَّ وَجَلَّ أَنْ يَرُدَّنِي لِمَا كُنْتُ

"Talk about Bani Israel, and there's no sin in that, as they experienced strange events." Then he began to say: "A group from amongst Bani Israel went out until they reached one of the graves of Bani Israel, and they said: 'If we were to pray two raka'at and ask Allah (Azza wa Jalla) to remove a man from those who had died, so that we may ask him about death.' So they did that and when they did it, a man raised his head from out of one of those graves; he was light brown skinned and had a prostration mark between his eyes. He said: 'What do you want with me? I died one hundred years ago and the heat of death wasn't soothed until recently. Ask Allah to return me to the way I was.'"[98]

[98] Reported by Imam Ahmad in "Az-Zuhud"; Ibn Abi Shaibah in "Al-Musannaf", without the story; and likewise, Al-Bazzar in his "Musnad". Sheikh Al-Albani (rahimahullah) said in "As-Silsilah As-Sahihah", number: 2926: "This is a chain of narration with trustworthy narrators."

87. It is related from Anas bin Malik (radiallahu anhu) that the Messenger of Allah (sallallahu alaihi wa sallam) said:

إِذَا وَلِيَ أَحَدُكُمْ أَخَاهُ ، فَلْيُحْسِنْ كَفَنَهُ ، فَإِنَّهُمْ يُبْعَثُونَ فِي أَكْفَانِهِمْ ، وَ يَتَزَاوَرُونَ فِي أَكْفَانِهِمْ

"If any of you is entrusted with his brother (i.e., his funeral), then make his shroud a good one, as they will be resurrected in their shroud and they visit one another in their shrouds."[99]

88. It is related that Abu Burdah said: "I came to Medina and Abdullah bin Umar came to me and said:

أَ تَدْرِي لِمَ أَتَيْتُكَ ؟ قَالَ : لَا . قَالَ : سَمِعْتُ رَسُولَ اللهِ - صَلَّى اللهُ عَلَيْهِ وَ سَلَّمَ - يَقُولُ : ((مَنْ أَحَبَّ أَنْ يَصِلَ أَبَاهُ فِي قَبْرِهِ ، فَلْيَصِلْ إِخْوَانَ أَبِيهِ بَعْدَهُ)).

'Do you know why I have come to you?' I said: 'No;' he said: 'I heard the Messenger of Allah say: 'Whoever wants to do a kindness to their father that is in his grave, then let him do a kindness to his father's brothers (i.e., close friends) after him.' And there was, between my father and yours,

[99] Reported by Al-Khatib in his "Tarikh". Sheikh Al-Albani (rahimahullah) said in "As-Silsilah As-Sahihah", number: 1425: "It is authentic due to supporting narrations.

brotherhood and love, so I wanted to do a kindness for you.'"[100]

---

[100] Reported by Abu Ya'la and Ibn Hibban, number: 2031. Sheikh Al-Albani (rahimahullah) said in "As-Silsilah As-Sahihah", number: 1432: "An authentic chain of narration in accordance with Al-Bukhari's standards."

CHAPTER 12: THE DECEASED'S AWARENESS OF SOME OF THE AFFAIRS OF THE LIVING

89. It is related that Amr bin Hazm (radiallahu anhu) said:

رَآنِي رَسُولُ اللهِ - صَلَّى اللهُ عَلَيْهِ وَ سَلَّمَ - عَلَى قَبْرٍ، فَقَالَ : ((انْزِلْ عَنِ الْقَبْرِ ، لَا تُؤْذِش صَاحِبَ هَذَا الْقَبْرِ)).

"The Messenger of Allah (sallallahu alaihi wa sallam) saw me on top of a grave, so he said: 'Get off that grave. Don't harm the resident of this grave!'"[101]

90. It is related that Bashir bin Al-Khasasiyah (radiallahu anhu) said that the Messenger of Allah (sallallahu alaihi wa sallam) came to some Muslim graves and he said:

لَقَدْ أَدْرَكَ هَؤُلَاءِ خَيْرًا كَثِيرًا (ثَلَاثَ مَرَّاتٍ). فَبَيْنَمَا هُوَ يَمْشِي ، إِذْ حَانَتْ مِنْهُ نَظْرَةٌ ، فَإِذَا هُوَ بِرَجُلٍ يَمْشِي بَيْنَ الْقُبُورِ ، عَلَيْهِ نَعْلَانِ ، فَقَالَ : ((يَا

[101] Reported by Ahmad, Abu Nu'aim in "Ma'rifatus Sahabah", Ibn Al-Athir in "Asad Al-Ghabah", and Ibn Asakir in "Tarikh Dimashq". Sheikh Al-Albani (rahimahullah) said in "As-Silsilah As-Sahihah", number: 2960: "Its chain of narration is authentic, and its narrators are trustworthy."

صَاحِبَ السِّبْتِيَّتَيْنِ ، وَيْحَكَ ! أَلْقِ سِبْتِيَّتَيْكَ)) .

فَنَظَرَ ، فَلَمَّا عَرَفَ الرَّجُلُ رَسُولَ اللهِ - صَلَّى اللهُ عَلَيْهِ

وَ سَلَّمَ ، خَلَعَ نَعْلَهُ ، فَرَمَى بِهِمَا .

"Indeed, these people attained much good." Three times. Then as he was walking, his eyes happened to fall on a man walking between the graves wearing shoes, so he said: "Oh you wearing the shoes, woe unto you! Remove your shoes!" The man looked over and when he realized it was the Messenger of Allah, he took off his shoes and threw them away.[102]

91. It is related that Abdullah bin Umar (radiallahu anhu) said that the Prophet (sallallahu alaihi wa sallam) looked at the people of the well (the well in which the bodies of the pagans killed in the Battle of Badr were thrown) and said,

وَجَدْتُمْ مَا وَعَدَ رَبُّكُمْ حَقًّا ؟ فَقِيلَ لَهُ : تَدْعُو أَمْوَاتًا

؟! فَقَالَ : ((مَا أَنْتُمْ بِأَسْمَعَ مِنْهُمْ ، وَ لَكِنْ لَا

يُجِيبُونَ)) .

---

[102] Reported by At-Tiyaalisi, Ahmad, Abu Dawud, Ibn Majah, Ibn Abi Shaibah, At-Tabarani, Al-Hakim, and Al-Bayhaqi. Reported as it is in "Ahkam Al-Jana'iz" by Al-Albani (rahimahullah), page: 173, paragraph: 88. Sheikh Muqbil Al-Wadi'i declared it authentic in "Al-Jami' As-Sahih" (2/279-280).

"Have you found true what your Lord promised you?" Somebody said to him, "You are addressing dead people." He replied, "You do not hear any better than they do, but they cannot reply."[103]

92. It is related that A'ishah (radiallahu anha) said that the Prophet (sallallahu alaihi wa sallam) said regarding the people thrown in the well:

إِنَّهُمْ لَيَعْلَمُونَ الْآنَ، أَنَّ مَا كُنْتُ أَقُولُ لَهُمْ حَقٌّ.

"They now realize that what I used to tell them was the truth."[104]

93. It is related that Abu Hurairah (radiallahu anhu) said that the Messenger of Allah said:

---

[103] Reported by Al-Bukhari, number: 1304; and Muslim, number: 932. Al-Bukhari mentioned it in "Kitabul Jana'iz", Section: "What Came Regarding the Punishment of the Grave," section number: 85.

[104] Reported by Al-Bukhari, number: 1305; and Muslim, number: 932. Muslim reported it alone by way of Anas, number: 2874. Muslim also reported it alone by way of Umar, number: 2873. Al-Bukhari reported it (i.e., the Hadith of the People thrown in the well), number: 3757; and Muslim, number: 2875, by way of Abu Talha.

لَأَنْ يَجْلِسَ أَحَدُكُمْ عَلَى جَمْرَةٍ، فَتُحْرِقَ ثِيَابَهُ، فَتَخْلُصَ إِلَى جِلْدِهِ، خَيْرٌ لَهُ مِنْ أَنْ يَجْلِسَ عَلَى قَبْرٍ.

"It is better that one of you should sit on live coals which would burn his clothing through to his skin than that he should sit on a grave."[105]

94. It is related from Uqbah bin Amir (radiallahu anhu) that the Messenger of Allah (sallallahu alaihi wa sallam) said:

لَأَنْ أَمْشِيَ عَلَى جَمْرَةٍ، أَوْ سَيْفٍ، أَوْ أَخْصِفَ نَعْلِي بِرِجْلِي، أَحَبُّ إِلَيَّ مِنْ أَنْ أَمْشِيَ عَلَى قَبْرِ مُسْلِمٍ. وَ مَا أُبَالِي، أَوَسَطَ الْقُبُورِ قَضَيْتُ حَاجَتِي، أَوْ وَسَطَ السُّوقِ.

"It is more beloved to me to walk upon burning coals or a sword, or to sew shoes to my feet than to walk over a Muslim's grave. And there is no difference to me to relieve myself in the middle of

[105] Reported by Muslim, number: 971; Ahmad, Abu Dawud, An-Nisaa, and Ibn Majah. Sheikh Al-Albani declared it authentic in "Sahih Al-Jami'", number: 5042 and in "Sahih At-Targhib wat Tarhib", number: 3563.

the graveyard or in the middle of the market place."[106]

ℰ✹✹✹ℛ

---

[106] Reported by Ibn Majah, number: 1567. Sheikh Al-Albani (rahimahullah) declared it authentic in "Sahih Al-Jami'", number: 5038. And he said in "Sahih At-Targhib wat Tarhib", number: 3564: "(reported) with a 'good' chain of narration."

CHAPTER 13: THE STATE OF THE PROPHETS IN THEIR GRAVES

95. It is related that Ana's bin Malik (radiallahu anhu) said that the Messenger of Allah said:

الْأَنْبِيَاءُ صَلَوَاتُ اللهِ عَلَيْهِمْ ، أَحْيَاءُ فِي قُبُورِهِمْ ، يُصَلُّونَ .

"The prophets, may the blessings of Allah be upon them, are alive in their graves, praying."[107]

96. It is also related by him that the Messenger of Allah (sallallahu alaihi wa sallam) said:

مَرَرْتُ لَيْلَةَ أُسْرِيَ بِي عَلَى مُوسَى ، فَرَأَيْتُهُ قَائِمًا يُصَلِّي فِي قَبْرِهِ، عِنْدَ الْكَثِيبِ الْأَحْمَرِ

"On the night of my ascension, I passed by Musa and I saw him standing in prayer in his grave, at the red dune."[108]

---

[107] Reported by Al-Bazzar in his "Musnad", number: 256; Tammam Ar-Razi in his "Fawa'id", number: 56; Ibn Asakir in his "Tarikh"; Ibn Uday in his "Kamil"; and Al-Bayhaqi in "Juz Hayatul Anbiya", page 3. Sheikh Al-Albani (rahimahullah) mentioned it in "As-Silsilah As-Sahihah", number: 621.

[108] Reported by Muslim, number: 2375; An-Nisa'i, Ibn Hibban, and Ahmad. See: "As-Silsilah As-Sahihah", number: 262.

97. It is related that Abu Hurairah (radiallahu anhu) said that the Messenger of Allah (sallallahu alaihi wa sallam) said:

مَا مِنْ أَحَدٍ يُسَلِّمُ عَلَيَّ ، إِلَّا رَدَّ اللهُ عَلَيَّ رُوحِي ، حَتَّى أَرُدَّ عَلَيْهِ السَّلَامَ

"No one sends the salutations upon me, except that Allah returns my soul to me, so that I may reply the salutations."[109]

98. It is related that Abu Bakr As-Siddiq (radiallahu anhu) said that the Messenger of Allah (sallallahu alaihi wa sallam) said:

أَكْثِرُوا الصَّلَاةَ عَلَيَّ ، فَإِنَّ اللهَ وَكَّلَ بِي مَلَكًا عِنْدَ قَبْرِي ، فَإِذَا صَلَّى عَلَيَّ رَجُلٌ مِنْ أُمَّتِي ، قَالَ لِي ذَلِكَ الْمَلَكُ : يَا مُحَمَّدُ ، إِنَّ فُلَانَ بْنَ فُلَانٍ ، صَلَّى عَلَيْكَ السَّاعَةَ .

"Increase your salutations upon me, for Allah has entrusted an Angel with me to be by my grave, so if a person from my Ummah sends the salutations upon me, then the angel will say: 'O Muhammad! So

---

[109] Reported by Abu Dawud, number: 2041. Sheikh Al-Albani declared it to be "good" in "Sahih Abi Dawud", number: 2041, and in "Sahih Al-Jami'", number: 5679.

and so, son of so and so, just now sent the salutations upon you.'"[110]

99. It is related from Aws bin Aws (radiallahu anhu) that the Messenger of Allah (sallallahu alaihi wa sallam) said:

أَكْثِرُوا عَلَيَّ مِنَ الصَّلَاةِ يَوْمَ الْجُمْعَةِ، فَإِنَّ صَلَاتَكُمْ مَعْرُوضَةٌ عَلَيَّ. قَالُوا: كَيْفَ تُعْرَضُ عَلَيْكَ، وَ قَدْ أَرِمْتَ ؟! قَالَ: ((إِنَّ اللهَ تَعَالَى حَرَّمَ عَلَى الْأَرْضِ أَنْ تَأْكُلَ أَجْسَادَ الْأَنْبِيَاءِ)).

"Increase your salutations upon me on Jum'ah, for verily your salutations are presented to me." The people said: "How will they be presented to you when you have decomposed?" So he said: "Verily Allah, the Most High, has made it forbidden for the earth to eat away at the bodies of the Prophets."[111]

---

[110] Reported by Ad-Deelami. As it is reported in "As-Silsilah As-Sahihah" by Sheikh Al-Albani, number: 1530.

[111] Reported by Abu Dawud, number: 1047; An-Nisaa'i (1/91-92); Ibn Majah, numbers: 1636 and 1085; Ad-Darami, and Al-Bayhaqi in "Ad-Da'wat Al-Kabir" as it is reported in "Hadayatur Rawaat", number: 1310. Authenticated by Sheikh Al-Albani (rahimahullah) in "Sahih Sunan Abi Dawud", number: 1047; and see "Al-Mishkat", number: 1316. Sheikh Al-Albani (rahimahullah) said in "As-Silsilah As-Sahihah", number: 1527: "An authentic chain of narration."

CHAPTER 14: THE BELIEVER IN HIS GRAVE WISHES HE COULD HAVE INCREASED HIS GOOD DEEDS

100. It is related that Abu Hurairah said that the Prophet (sallallahu alaihi wa sallam) passed by a new grave, and he said:

رَكْعَتَانِ خَفِيفَتَانِ مِمَّا تَحْقِرُونَ ، وَ تَنَفَّلُونَ ، يَزِيدُهُمَا هَذَا - يُشِيرُ إِلَى قَبْرٍ - فِي عَمَلِهِ ، أَحَبُّ إِلَيْهِ مِنْ بَقِيَّةِ دُنْيَاكُمْ

> **"Two light rakaat of prayer, that you think little of and perform voluntarily, for this person (and he indicated towards the grave) to increase his actions with, is more beloved to him than the rest of your life in this world (is to you)."**[112]

101. It is related that Jabir bin Abdullah Al-Ansari (radiallahu anhu) said that the Prophet (sallallahu alaihi wa sallam) said:

---

112 Reported by Ibn Saa'id in "Zawa'id Az-Zuhd"; Abu Nu'aim in "Akhbar Asbahan"; and At-Tabarani in "Al-Awsat". Sheikh Al-Albani (rahimahullah) said in "As-Silsilah As-Sahihah", number: 1388: "An authentic chain of narration, to the standard of Muslim."

إِذَا دَخَلَ الْمَيِّتُ الْقَبْرَ، مُثِّلَتْ لَهُ الشَّمْسُ عِنْدَ غُرُوبِهَا، فَيَقُولُ: دَعُونِي أُصَلِّي.

"When the deceased enters the grave, the sun is made to appear as if it is setting, and he says: 'Let me pray.'"[113]

৩✹✹✹ଓ

[113] Reported by Ibn Hibban (7/385), checking by Shu'aib; Ibn Majah, number: 4272; and Ibn Abi Asim in "Kitab As-Sunnah", number: 867. Shu'aib Al-Arna'ut declared it to be "good".

CHAPTER 15: VISITING GRAVES

102. It is related that Buraidah (radiallahu anhu) said that the Prophet (sallallahu alaihi wa sallam) taught us that when we visit graves, we should say,

السَّلَامُ عَلَى أَهْلِ الدِّيَارِ - وَ فِي رِوَايَةٍ : السَّلَامُ عَلَيْكُمْ أَهْلَ الدِّيَارِ - مِنَ الْمُؤْمِنِينَ وَ الْمُسْلِمِينَ ، وَ إِنَّا إِنْ شَاءَ اللهُ لَلَاحِقُونَ ، أَسْأَلُ اللهَ لَنَا وَ لَكُمُ الْعَافِيَةَ .

"May peace be upon the dwellers of this place;" and in another narration: "May peace be upon you, O dwellers of this place, O believing men and women, certainly, Allah willing, we will join you. We supplicate to Allah to grant us and you well-being."[114]

---

[114] Reported by Muslim, number: 975.

CHAPTER 16: THE PREFERENCE OF CRYING AT THE GRAVE

103. It is related that Al-Bara bin Al-Aazab said:

بَيْنَا نَحْنُ مَعَ رَسُولِ اللهِ - صَلَّى اللهُ عَلَيْهِ وَ سَلَّمَ - إِذْ بَصُرَ بِجَمَاعَةٍ ، فَقَالَ : ((عَلَامَ اجْتَمَعَ عَلَيْهِ هَؤُلَاءِ ؟)) قِيلَ : عَلَى قَبْرٍ يَحْفِرُونَهُ . قَالَ : فَفَزِعَ رَسُولُ اللهِ - صَلَّى اللهُ عَلَيْهِ وَ سَلَّمَ - ، فَبَدَرَ بَيْنَ يَدَيْ أَصْحَابِهِ مُسْرِعًا ، حَتَّى انْتَهَى إِلَى الْقَبْرِ ، فَجَثَا عَلَيْهِ ، فَاسْتَقْبَلْتُهُ مِنْ بَيْنَ يَدَيْهِ ، لِأَنْظُرَ مَا يَصْنَعُ ، فَبَكَى ، حَتَّى بَلَّ الثَّرَى مِنْ دُمُوعِهِ ، ثُمَّ أَقْبَلَ عَلَيْنَا ، فَقَالَ : ((أَيْ إِخْوَانِي ، لِمِثْلِ الْيَوْمِ فَأَعِدُّوا)) .

"We were with the Messenger of Allah (sallallahu alaihi wa sallam), when he saw a group, so he said: 'Why are they gathering?' so it was said: 'They are digging a grave.' So he rushed through his companions until he came to the grave, and he knelt in front of it. I stood right in front of him to see what he was doing. He began to cry until the ground became wet from his tears. Then he turned to face us

and said: 'O my brothers, prepare yourselves for a day like this.'"[115]

104. It is related from Hani, the freed slave of Uthman, that he said:

إِذَا وَقَفَ عَلَى قَبْرٍ بَكَى حَتَّى يَبُلَّ لِحْيَتَهُ ، فَقِيلَ : تَذْكُرُ الْجَنَّةَ وَ النَّارَ وَ لَا تَبْكِي ، وَ تَبْكِي مِنْ هَذَا ؟! فَقَالَ : إِنَّ رَسُولَ اللهِ - صَلَّى اللهُ عَلَيْهِ وَ سَلَّمَ - قَالَ : ((إِنَّ الْقَبْرَ أَوَّلُ مَنْزِلٍ مِنْ مَنَازِلِ الْآخِرَةِ ، فَإِنْ نَجَا مِنْهُ ، فَمَا بَعْدَهُ أَيْسَرُ مِنْهُ ، وَ إِنْ لَمْ يَنْجُ مِنْهُ ، فَمَا بَعْدَهُ أَشَدُّ مِنْهُ)) قَالَ : وَ قَالَ رَسُولُ اللهِ - صَلَّى اللهُ عَلَيْهِ وَ سَلَّمَ - : ((مَا رَأَيْتُ مَنْظَرًا قَطُّ ، إِلَّا وَ الْقَبْرُ أَفْظَعُ مِنْهُ)) .

"When 'Uthman bin Affan stood beside a grave, he would weep until his beard became wet. It was said to him: 'You remember Paradise and Hell, and you do not weep, but you weep for this?' He said: 'The

[115] Reported by Al-Bukhari in "At-Tarikh"; Ibn Majah, number: 4195; Ahmad; Abu Bakr Ash-Shafi'i in "Majlasan"; Ar-Ruyani in his "Musnad", and Al-Khatib in his "Tarikh". Sheikh Al-Albani (rahimahullah) declared it to be "good" in "As-Silsilah As-Sahihah", number: 1751, and in "Sahih At-Targhib wat Tarhib", number: 3338.

Messenger of Allah (sallallahu alaihi wa sallam) said: 'The grave is the first stage of the Hereafter. Whoever is delivered from it, then what comes after it is easier. If he is not delivered from it, then what comes after it is harder." He said that the Messenger of Allah (sallallahu alaihi wa sallam) said: 'I have never seen a horrible sight except that the grave was worse.'"[116]

---

[116] Reported by At-Tirmidhi and Ibn Majah. At-Tirmidhi, Ibn Majah, and Al-Hakim also related this hadith by way of Abu Hurayrah. Sheikh Al-Albani (rahimahullah) declared it to be "good" in "Sahih Al-Jami'", number: 5623. Sheikh Muqbil (rahimahullah) declared it authentic in "Sahih Al-Jami' mimma Laisa fis Sahihain" (2/71) and in "Al-Jami' As-Sahih" (2/275).

CHAPTER 17: THE BELIEFS OF AHLUS SUNNAH WAL JAMA'AH REGARDING THE PUNISHMENT AND PLEASURE OF THE GRAVE

Imam At-Tahawi (rahimahullah) said in "Aqidah At-Tahawiyah", pages: 390 and 396:

> "We believe in the Angel of Death, whom is entrusted with the taking of the souls of the creation; the punishment of the grave for the one that is deserving of that; Munkar's and Nakir's questioning in his grave..."

The Scholar of Islam, Ibn Taymiyyah (rahimahullah) said[117]:

> "Belief in the Hereafter involves belief in everything that the Prophet (sallallahu alaihi wa sallam) informed us of concerning what will come after death, so he (the Muslim) believes in the trials of the grave and the punishment and pleasure of the grave.
>
> "In terms of the trial, then the people will be tested in their graves. So it will be said to a man: 'Who is your Lord? What is your religion? Who is your Prophet?' Allah will make those that believed in the *Firm*

---

[117] in "Aqidah Wasatiyah", as was checked by Zuhair Ash-Shawish, and printed by Al-Maktab Al-Islami, page: 4039.

> *Statement* in this life and the Hereafter firm, so the believer will say: 'Allah is my Lord, Islam is my religion, and Muhammad is my Prophet.' The doubtful person, on the other hand, will say: 'Umm, umm, I don't know. I heard the people say something, so I said it too.' Then he will be struck with a hammer made of steel, and he will scream a scream so loud that everything will hear him, except mankind, and if they could hear it, they would collapse.
>
> "Then after this trial, there will either be pleasure or punishment lasting until the Last Day is established and the souls are returned to their bodies."

Ibn Abi Al-Izz said[118]:

> "The number of narrations from the Messenger of Allah that affirm the punishment and pleasure of the grave for whoever is deserving of that, reached a level that confirms its authenticity beyond a reasonable doubt, as well as the questioning of the two angels. Therefore, belief in the existence of these things and faith in it is obligatory..."

The great scholar Ibn Uthaimeen said in "Sharh Al-Aqidah Al-Wasatiyyah" at Sheikh Ibn Taymiyyah's statement regarding the punishment and pleasure of the grave:

> "There is in it the affirmation of the pleasure and punishment in the grave, and Allah's Book and the

---

118 in "Sharh Al-Aqidah At-Tahawiyyah", page: 399.

> Sunnah of His Messenger prove this; in fact, we can also state the Ijma' (consensus) of the Muslims."

From the book "Nathmul Mutanathir min Al-Hadith Al-Mutawatir" by Al-Katani, page: 38, under the chapter: "What was Narrated Concerning the Punishment of the Grave," he wrote:

> "Al-Qadi Iyad said: 'It reached a level of reporters by which its authenticity is beyond a reasonable doubt and Ahlus Sunnah (the People of Prophetic Narrations) have reached consensus concerning it.' and the author of "Al-Masabih" said: 'If nothing of the punishment of the grave is true then nothing in the religion is true.' and he said: 'It reached a level of reporters by which its authenticity is beyond a reasonable doubt and was reported by more than 30 companions.'"

A BENEFIT

Ibn Al-Qayyim (rahimahullah) said[119]:

> "Issue Eight: Is the statement of the questioner: 'What is the wisdom behind the fact the punishment in the grave is not mentioned in the Quran, considering the extreme need to know about it and believe in it, to warn people and to allow people to protect themselves from it?'

"The answer is from two viewpoints: the summary view and the detailed view.

> "In terms of the summary viewpoint: Allah, the Glorified, the Most High, revealed to His Prophet (sallallahu alaihi wa sallam) two forms of revelation: the Book and the Wisdom. He, the Most High, said:
>
> ﴿وَأَنزَلَ ٱللَّهُ عَلَيۡكَ ٱلۡكِتَٰبَ وَٱلۡحِكۡمَةَ﴾
>
> **'And Allah sent down upon you the Book and the Wisdom.'** [120]
>
> And He, the Most High, said:
>
> ﴿هُوَ ٱلَّذِي بَعَثَ فِي ٱلۡأُمِّيِّـۧنَ رَسُولٗا مِّنۡهُمۡ يَتۡلُواْ عَلَيۡهِمۡ ءَايَٰتِهِۦ وَيُزَكِّيهِمۡ
> وَيُعَلِّمُهُمُ ٱلۡكِتَٰبَ وَٱلۡحِكۡمَةَ﴾

---

119 in his book "Ar-Ruh", the Muhammad Ali Subaih Print, page: 110-113.

120 Soorah An-Nisaa (4:113)

'He it is Who sent among the unlettered ones a messenger from among themselves, reciting to them His verses, purifying them, and teaching them the Book and the Wisdom. And verily, they had been in manifest error.' [121]

And He, the Most High, said:

﴿ وَٱذْكُرْنَ مَا يُتْلَىٰ فِى بُيُوتِكُنَّ مِنْ ءَايَٰتِ ٱللَّهِ وَٱلْحِكْمَةِ ﴾

'And remember, that which is recited in your houses of Allah's verses and the Wisdom.' [122]

"The Book is the Quran and the Wisdom is the Sunnah, by agreement of the Salaf (predecessors). Whatever the Prophet (sallallahu alaihi wa sallam) informed about Allah, it is obligatory to affirm and believe in it, just as it is for that which Allah informed of upon the tongue of His messenger. This is a principle agreed upon by all Muslims and only those not from amongst them deny it. The Prophet (sallallahu alaihi wa sallam) said: 'Indeed, I brought the Book and the likes of it with it.'

"In terms of the detailed viewpoint: then the pleasure and punishment of Al-Barzakh is mentioned in the Quran, in more than one place, from amongst them is His, the Most High's, statement:

---

[121] Soorah Jum'ah (62: 2)

[122] Soorah Al-Ahzab (33: 34)

﴿ وَلَوْ تَرَىٰٓ إِذِ ٱلظَّٰلِمُونَ فِى غَمَرَٰتِ ٱلْمَوْتِ وَٱلْمَلَٰٓئِكَةُ بَاسِطُوٓا۟ أَيْدِيهِمْ أَخْرِجُوٓا۟ أَنفُسَكُمُ ۖ ٱلْيَوْمَ تُجْزَوْنَ عَذَابَ ٱلْهُونِ بِمَا كُنتُمْ تَقُولُونَ عَلَى ٱللَّهِ غَيْرَ ٱلْحَقِّ وَكُنتُمْ عَنْ ءَايَٰتِهِۦ تَسْتَكْبِرُونَ ﴿٩٣﴾ ﴾

'And if you could but see when the oppressors are in the agonies of death, while the angels are stretching forth their hands (saying): 'Deliver your souls! This day you shall be recompensed with the torment of degradation because of what you used to utter against Allah other than the truth. And you used to reject His verses!''[123]

"This was an address to them at the time of death and the Angels, who are truthful, informed that at that time, they will be recompensed with a torment of degradation. If that was delayed until the end of the Dunya then it would not be correct to say "today you will be recompensed."

"Also from the verses that describe Al-Barzakh is His, the Most High's, statement:

﴿ فَوَقَىٰهُ ٱللَّهُ سَيِّـَٔاتِ مَا مَكَرُوا۟ ۖ وَحَاقَ بِـَٔالِ فِرْعَوْنَ سُوٓءُ ٱلْعَذَابِ ﴿٤٥﴾ ٱلنَّارُ يُعْرَضُونَ عَلَيْهَا غُدُوًّا وَعَشِيًّا ۖ وَيَوْمَ تَقُومُ ٱلسَّاعَةُ أَدْخِلُوٓا۟ ءَالَ فِرْعَوْنَ أَشَدَّ ٱلْعَذَابِ ﴿٤٦﴾ ﴾

123 Soorah Al-An'am (6: 93)

'So Allah saved him from the evils that they plotted (against him), while an evil torment encompassed Pharoah's people. The Fire; they are exposed to it, morning and afternoon, and on the Day when the Hour will be established (it will be said to the angels): 'Cause Pharaoh's people to enter the severest torment!"[124]

"So, the punishment of the two realms (this life and the Hereafter) is mentioned clearly so that it could not be possibly anything else.

"Also from these verses is His, the Most High's, statement:

﴿ فَذَرْهُمْ حَتَّىٰ يُلَٰقُوا۟ يَوْمَهُمُ ٱلَّذِى فِيهِ يُصْعَقُونَ ﴿٤٥﴾ يَوْمَ لَا يُغْنِى عَنْهُمْ كَيْدُهُمْ
شَيْـًٔا وَلَا هُمْ يُنصَرُونَ ﴿٤٦﴾ وَإِنَّ لِلَّذِينَ ظَلَمُوا۟ عَذَابًا دُونَ ذَٰلِكَ وَلَٰكِنَّ أَكْثَرَهُمْ لَا
يَعْلَمُونَ ﴿٤٧﴾ ﴾

'So leave them alone till they meet their Day, in which they will collapse (in horror). The Day when their plotting shall not avail them at all nor will they be helped. And verily, for those who do wrong, there is another punishment before this, but most of them know not.' [125]

This verse could possibly mean the punishment of murder, for example, in the Dunya, or the punishment of Al-Barzakh, and the latter is more

---

[124] Soorah Al-Ghafir (40: 45-46)
[125] Soorah At-Tur (52: 45-47)

likely, as most of them died and were not punished in their lifetimes. It could also be said, and this is even more likely, that those of them that had died were punished in Al-Barzakh, and those that remained were punished in the Dunya by murder or other things. So it is a threat of punishment in the Dunya and in Al-Barzakh.

﴿ وَلَنُذِيقَنَّهُم مِّنَ ٱلْعَذَابِ ٱلْأَدْنَىٰ دُونَ ٱلْعَذَابِ ٱلْأَكْبَرِ لَعَلَّهُمْ يَرْجِعُونَ ﴿٢١﴾ ﴾

"And from these verses is His, the Most High's, statement: 'And verily, We will make them taste some of the minor torment prior to the major torment, in order that they may return.'[126]

"A number of people used this verse as a proof for the punishment of the grave, such as Abdullah bin Al-Abbas, and there is some substance to it, because this punishment in the Dunya calls for them to return from their disbelief, and this was not hidden from the "Scholar of the Ummah" and the "Explainer of the Quran," but with his understanding of the Quran and his precise comprehension of it, he understood it to be the punishment of the grave, because Allah, the Glorified, informed that He has for them two punishments: one major and one minor. Allah informs that He makes the disbelievers taste some of the minor punishment so that they may return to

---

126 Soorah As-Sajdah (32: 21).

belief. Therefore, this indicates that there remains some of the minor punishment for them to be punished after the punishment of the Dunya. This is why He said: 'some of the minor torment' and not 'And verily, We will make them taste the minor torment,' so consider this. And this is similar to the Prophet's saying: 'So a window will be opened for him to the Hellfire, and some of its heat and hot winds are brought to him.' and he did not say 'and its heat and hot wind are brought to him.' Therefore, that which reaches him is a portion of that, but more remains. Those that taste some of the punishment are the enemies of Allah, and there still remains for them a punishment that is much greater.

﴿ فَلَوْلَآ إِذَا بَلَغَتِ ٱلْحُلْقُومَ (٨٣) وَأَنتُمْ حِينَئِذٍ تَنظُرُونَ (٨٤) وَنَحْنُ أَقْرَبُ إِلَيْهِ
مِنكُمْ وَلَٰكِن لَّا تُبْصِرُونَ (٨٥) فَلَوْلَآ إِن كُنتُمْ غَيْرَ مَدِينِينَ (٨٦) تَرْجِعُونَهَآ إِن
كُنتُمْ صَٰدِقِينَ (٨٧) فَأَمَّآ إِن كَانَ مِنَ ٱلْمُقَرَّبِينَ (٨٨) فَرَوْحٌ وَرَيْحَانٌ وَجَنَّتُ نَعِيمٍ
(٨٩) وَأَمَّآ إِن كَانَ مِنْ أَصْحَٰبِ ٱلْيَمِينِ (٩٠) فَسَلَٰمٌ لَّكَ مِنْ أَصْحَٰبِ ٱلْيَمِينِ (٩١)
وَأَمَّآ إِن كَانَ مِنَ ٱلْمُكَذِّبِينَ ٱلضَّآلِّينَ (٩٢) فَنُزُلٌ مِّنْ حَمِيمٍ (٩٣) وَتَصْلِيَةُ جَحِيمٍ
(٩٤) إِنَّ هَٰذَا لَهُوَ حَقُّ ٱلْيَقِينِ (٩٥) فَسَبِّحْ بِٱسْمِ رَبِّكَ ٱلْعَظِيمِ (٩٦) ﴾

"Also from amongst the verses that mention punishment of the grave is His, the Most High's, saying: 'Then why do you not (intervene) when (the soul of a dying person) reaches the throat? And you at the moment are looking on. But We (i.e., Our

angels who take the soul) are nearer to him than you, but you see not. Then why do you not, if you are exempt (from the reckoning and recompense), bring back the soul (to its body), if you are truthful? Then, if he (the dying person) is from those brought near (to Allah), (then for him is) rest and provision, and a Garden of delights (Paradise). And if he (the dying person) be of those on the Right Hand, then there is safety and peace for those on the Right Hand. But if he is from the deniers (of the Resurrection), the misguided, then for him is entertainment with boiling water, and burning in Hell-fire. Verily, this is a certain truth. So glorify with praises the Name of your Lord, the Most Great.'[127]

"Here, Allah mentions the rulings of the souls at the time of death, and He mentions at the beginning of the Surah the Day of the Great Return and He mentioned that first to indicate its importance, since it is more important and more deserving of mentioning. Allah puts the souls into three categories at the time of death, just as they will be of three types in the Hereafter.

"Also from the verses mentioning Al-Barzakh is His, the Most High's, statement:

﴿ يَـٰٓأَيَّتُهَا ٱلنَّفْسُ ٱلْمُطْمَئِنَّةُ ﴿٢٧﴾ ٱرْجِعِىٓ إِلَىٰ رَبِّكِ رَاضِيَةً مَّرْضِيَّةً ﴿٢٨﴾ فَٱدْخُلِى فِى عِبَـٰدِى ﴿٢٩﴾ وَٱدْخُلِى جَنَّتِى ﴿٣٠﴾ ﴾

127 Soorah Al-Waqi'ah (56: 83-96).

'O restful soul! Come back to your Lord, well-pleased and well-pleasing unto Him! Enter amongst My (honored) slaves. And enter My Paradise!'[128]

"The Salaf have differed about when this will be said to the soul. One group says it will be said to him at the time of death, and the apparent meaning of the wording supports this view, as it is an address to the soul that has been separated and removed from the body; and this is how the Prophet (sallallahu alaihi wa sallam) explained the verse with his statement in Al-Baraa's hadith: 'It will be said to him: 'Come out pleased and well-pleased with.'' And this will follow in greater detail when the souls in Al-Barzakh is mentioned independently, if Allah wills.

"His, the Most High's, saying:

'Enter amongst My (honored) slaves' corresponds with his (sallallahu alaihi wa sallam) saying: 'O Allah, (make me from amongst) the highest of companions (in the hereafter).' If you were to consider the hadith about the punishment and pleasure of the grave you would find that they elaborate and explain the Quran. And by way of Allah is the success."

Ibn Al-Qayyim (rahimahullah) said[129]:

"Is the punishment of the grave on the soul and the body, or on the soul and not the body, or on the body and not the soul? And does the body share in the

---

[128] (Al-Fajr: 27-30).

[129] in his book "Ar-Ruh", the Muhammad Ali Subaih Print, page: 74-76.

> pleasure and punishments of the grave with the soul, or not?"

The Sheikh of Islam was asked about this issue and we remember the wording of his answer, he said:

> "The punishment and the pleasure are on the soul and body together by agreement of Ahlus Sunnah wal Jama'ah. The soul is given bliss or is punished separately from the body, and the soul is given bliss or is punished whilst connected to the body and the body connected to it, so the pleasure and torment of it whilst in this state is upon both of them, just as it is on the soul while it is separated from the body."

Is the punishment and bliss for the body and not the soul? There are two famous opinions from the People of Hadith and Sunnah and Ahlul Kalam (People of Rhetoric), and there are anomalous opinions, not from the opinions of the People of Hadith. For example: the opinion of those that say that the pleasure or the punishment only happens to the soul, and the body does not receive pleasure or punishment. This is said by the philosophers that deny the resurrection of the bodies. They are disbelievers by consensus of the Muslims. Many of the People of Rhetoric from amongst the Mu'tazilah and others are also of this opinion. They are the ones that acknowledge the resurrection of the bodies, but they say: that is not in Al-Barzakh; that is only at the time of being raised from the graves. They only deny the punishment of the body in Al-Barzakh and they say that it is the soul that is punished or given bliss, then when the last hour is established, the soul and body will be punished together.

This opinion is held by some of the Muslims from amongst the People of Rhetoric, the People of Hadith and others, and it is the choice of Ibn Hazm and Ibn Murra. This opinion is not from the three anomalous opinions, rather, it is connected to the opinion of those that believe in the punishment of the grave, acknowledge the Day of Judgment, and affirm the resurrection of the bodies and souls. This group has three opinions regarding the punishment of the grave:

The first: that the punishment occurs to the soul only.

The second: that the punishment happens to the soul and the body, by way of the soul.

The third: that it occurs only on the body.

In addition to that is the second opinion and that is the opinion of those that affirm the punishment of the grave but regard the soul to be life force. The anomalous opinions are of those who completely deny the punishment of the bodies or completely deny the punishment of the soul. Therefore, there are three anomalous opinions as the second opinion is also anomalous, i.e., the opinion of those that say that the soul does not experience the bliss nor is punished, as the soul is only the life force. And this is the opinion of some of the groups of the People of Rhetoric from amongst the Mu'tazilah, and Ash'ariyah, like Al-Qadi Abu Bakr and others, who deny the continuance of the soul after it is separated from the body. This opinion is void, and a number of his companions disagreed with him on this, like Abu Al-Ma'ali Al-Juwaini and others. In fact it is affirmed by Quran and the Sunnah that the soul does remain after it is separated from the body and that it is given bliss or it is punished. The divinity philosophers acknowledge that but deny the resurrection of the bodies, whilst those from the Mu'tazilah and Ash'ariyah acknowledge the resurrection of the bodies but deny the resurrection of the soul, or its pleasure or punishment without the body. Both of these opinions are wrong and misguided, but the opinion of the philosophers is further from the opinion of the people of Islam, even if those that agree with them believe that they are practicing Muslims or they believe that they are from amongst the people of knowledge, mysticism, investigation, and rhetoric.

The third anomalous opinion is the saying of those that say there is no pleasure or punishment in Al-Barzakh; in fact, that will not occur until the great hour is established. Therefore, they are similar to those from amongst the Mu'tazilah, and their like, that deny the punishment and pleasure of the grave, based on their view that the soul does not remain after its separation from the body, and that the body is not pleasured or tormented. So all of these groups are misguided regarding the issue of Al-Barzakh, but they are not all better than the philosophers, as they believe in the Great Resurrection.

So, if you know these false opinions, then also know the opinion of the Salaf of this Ummah and its leaders: when a person dies, he is in bliss or torment and that occurs to his soul and body, and that the soul continues, after it is separated from the body, to be pleasured or punished and that it is sometimes connected to the body. And that the punishment or pleasure happens to the body also with the soul. Then when the Great Day of Judgment is established, the souls will be returned to their bodies and they will raise from their graves for the Lord of creation.

The resurrection is something agreed upon by the Muslims, the Jews, and the Christians.

CONCLUSION

I ask Allah, the Great, to benefit Islam and the Muslims with this book and to add it to my measure of good deeds on the Day of Judgment, and to aid the truth and its people and to nullify the falsehood and its people.

I ask Allah to save us from punishment of the grave and the punishment of the fire, and we ask Him for Firdaus, the highest level of Paradise, the everlasting abode.

May Allah bless our Prophet, Muhammad, his family, and his companions, and grant them great peace.

تم بحمد الله